BLACK NATURE

Black

Nature

FOUR CENTURIES OF AFRICAN AMERICAN NATURE POETRY

EDITED BY CAMILLE T. DUNGY

The University of Georgia Press | Athens and London

Excerpt from 12 *Million Black Voices* © 1941 by Richard Wright.
Reprinted by permission of John Hawkins & Associates, Inc. Other credits
for previously published works appear on pages 351–360 and constitute
an extension of this copyright page.

© 2009 by the University of Georgia Press
Athens, Georgia 30602
www.ugapress.org
Set in Minion and Meta by Graphic Composition, Inc.

Printed digitally in the United States of America

Library of Congress Cataloging-in-Publication Data
Black nature : four centuries of African American nature
poetry / edited by Camille T. Dungy.
        p.   cm.
    Includes index.
    ISBN-13: 978-0-8203-3277-2 (cloth : alk. paper)
    ISBN-10: 0-8203-3277-1 (cloth : alk. paper)
    ISBN-13: 978-0-8203-3431-8 (pbk. : alk. paper)
    ISBN-10: 0-8203-3431-6 (pbk. : alk. paper)
    1. Nature—Poetry. 2. American poetry—African American authors.
3. American poetry—African American authors—History and criticism.
I. Dungy, Camille T., 1972–
    PS591.N4B49 2009
    808.81'936—dc22   2009018528

British Library Cataloging- in- Publication Data available

For Sunshine.

And in memory of Reginald Shepherd
and the many more we miss.
Your poems bloom—beautiful!—
within and beyond the margins of this book.

surely i am able to write poems
celebrating grass and how the blue
in the sky can flow green or red
and the waters lean against the
chesapeake shore like a familiar
poems about nature and landscape
surely   but whenever i begin
"the trees wave their knotted branches
and . . ."   why
is there under that poem always
an other poem?

—Lucille Clifton

CONTENTS

Cycle Three: Dirt on Our Hands

Cycle Eight: What the Land Remembers

ACKNOWLEDGMENTS

To the administration, faculty, and students of San Francisco State University, its College of Humanities, and its Creative Writing Department, my deepest gratitude for the financial, creative, and intellectual support that helped make this book possible.

Enduring appreciation to Randall Burkett, curator of Emory University's African American Collection; Stewart Shaw, African American Center Librarian at the San Francisco Public Library; and the librarians and curators at San Francisco State University, Stanford University, the University of California, Berkeley, and all the other collections that take African American literature seriously.

Thanks to the University of Georgia Press for the vision and tenacity to bring this book into the world.

For their assistance and discernment, I am deeply grateful to Lucy Anderton, Ray Black, Andrew Berzanskis, Shane Book, Dr. Robert Chrisman, Sebastian Matthews, Dr. Evie Shockley, Laura-Gray Street, Afaa Michael Weaver, Dr. Fredrick Woodard, and all the poets, editors, and readers who encouraged this project from its inception.

This book is for all of you.

THE NATURE OF AFRICAN AMERICAN POETRY

Camille T. Dungy

The first tree whose story I cared to discover grows through the filtration pumps at the edge of an abandoned swimming pool in a Lynchburg, Virginia, city park. In the late 1960s, a group of black children and community leaders staged a swim-in at this pool. Rather than desegregate this public facility, the city drained the water and replaced it with dirt. The space is now more lawn than pool. A gentle slope of lush grass reaches toward the deep end, and moss coats exposed walkways. A stately box elder grows through the retaining wall, roots ensnared in the pool's filtration system. This is the final insult. No child, black or white, will ever swim in this pool again. Thanks to the tree's tenacity, its remarkable, beautiful, uncompromised growth, the mechanisms that accommodated this simple form of recreation have been destroyed.

I discovered that pool and tree while adjusting to living in the South. Not a month into my tenure at a college in Lynchburg, I found myself walking with one of my new colleagues because we had both declined to drive the three-quarters of a mile from our small brick-walled campus to the president's residence for a reception for the poet laureate. Having just moved from Boston, I found I wasn't walking nearly enough. I tried to take any opportunity I could to get outside and stretch my legs, but walking seemed to be frowned upon in this southern town. "It's too hot," one member of the faculty had said. "Don't you want a ride to the reception? I've got air conditioning in my car," offered another. The New American South is a byproduct of air conditioning. Its denizens returned or stayed once the brutal climate could be tamed. No longer are residents dependent on open verandahs and tree-lined avenues to cool their homes. New subdivisions in the South are virtually indistinguishable from new subdivisions anywhere else in America, lots of lawns and few trees. Even as air conditioning has encouraged a reversal of the century-old patterns of northern migration, it has also continued the process of alienation from natural landscapes and environments. But the college that brought me to Virginia was in the old part of town, where the historical landscaping was well established. Streets were still tree-shaded and houses often nested in small, cooling groves. All those trees along the route overwhelmed me. I complained to my walking mate that, in addition to being frustrated by the lack of physical exercise available to me in this little town, I found myself understimulated creatively: "In Boston, I could look out the window and see people, people, people. So many stories to discover." I told her that when I first moved into my little house in Lynchburg, I thought there was nothing to see at all; "Now, I look out my window and see nothing but trees."

Then I discovered the tree in the pool and sought out the story behind it. Once I learned its history and its connection to the history of the town, I began to notice more and more moments of interactions between the human and nonhuman worlds, the Old and New South, and culturally and racially informed views of the natural world. Lynchburg had finally invested in new city pools because too many children, both black and white, were drowning in the city's many creeks and streams. I took my walks along these streams and noticed the daily changes in their currents. Suck holes and eddies appeared where there had been nothing but placid water the day before. I observed these deep pools of water and kept my eyes open for water moccasins or any of Virginia's three species of poisonous snakes. Although I never saw a single one, my attention was rewarded with beauty: blooming jack-in-the-pulpit nearly hidden on a heavily foliated embankment; a doe standing silent just off the trail, wise-eyed and protective of her fawn; beavers busy constructing a new dam. With the first autumn rains, their dam held fast. Their work meant my path was blocked by the flood. Diverted, I was unconcerned because in whichever direction I went there was plenty to see, plenty to learn, plenty to engage my creative attentions.

I bought nature guides and learned to identify leafless trees in winter. I walked daily and charted the calendar by the cyclical progress of leaves and buds and blossoms. I fell for flowers. Noting the crowning of the crocus and the budding of the forsythia, I became aware of how they foretold the swift onset of spring. I started writing about the landscape where I lived, and I began to pay more attention to what I remembered about the then-semi-rural Southern California landscape of my earlier years. Separated by many years and a wide continent from the environment of my childhood, I remembered a time and place where I felt immensely comfortable moving in and through the natural world. Though I had distanced myself from the necessity of that communion, my time in Virginia allowed me to begin to remember the ways and the reasons why I had once felt so comfortable outside. As much as the trees of the American South reminded me of a history steeped in often arbitrarily brutal and always dehumanizing racism, they also helped teach me how to make myself at home.

This anthology of black writers writing about the natural world is rooted in trees—in lush leaves and flowering branches. My developing appreciation of trees correlates to what I hope can be accomplished through the creative and critical responses to the poems and essays that make up this collection. In the same way my personal journey with the pool and its tree led me from indifference to intrigued observation, to an engagement with the devastating realities of history, and finally into a space of renewed connection to the natural world, the collective voice in this collection cycles through the spectrum of alignment with worlds beyond the human. This book, my own experience, investigations of African American literary engagement with the natural world: branches from one tree.

For years, poets and critics have called for a broader inclusiveness in conversations about ecocriticism and ecopoetics, one that acknowledges other voices and a wider range of cultural and ethnic concerns. African Americans, specifically, are fundamental to the natural fabric of this nation but have been noticeably absent from tables of contents. To bring more voices into the conversation about human interactions with the natural world, we must change the parameters of the conversation.

The poems and essays collected here serve as an introduction to a new way of thinking about nature writing and writing by black Americans. The traditional context of the nature poem in the Western intellectual canon, spawned by the likes of Virgil and Theocritus and solidified by the Romantics and Transcendentalists, informs the prevailing views of the natural world as a place of positive collaboration, refuge, idyllic rural life, or wilderness. The poetry of African Americans only conforms to these traditions in limited ways. Many black writers simply do not look at their environment from the same perspective as Anglo-American writers who discourse with the natural world. The pastoral as diversion, a construction of a culture that dreams, through landscape and animal life, of a certain luxury or innocence, is less prevalent. Rather, in a great deal of African American poetry we see poems written from the perspective of the workers of the field. Though these poems defy the pastoral conventions of Western poetry, are they not pastorals? The poems describe moss, rivers, trees, dirt, caves, dogs, fields: elements of an environment steeped in a legacy of violence, forced labor, torture, and death.

Are these not meditations on nature? We find poems set in urban streets. Can these not be landscape poems? The natural world, aligned with or in opposition to the human world, mediates the poems of this anthology. The poems reveal histories stored in various natural bodies. They document natural and human-provoked disasters and their effects on individuals and communities. They explore sources of connection to, but also alienation from, the land.

African Americans are tied up in the toil and soil involved in working this land into the country we know today. Viewed once as chattel, part of a farm's livestock or an asset in a banker's ledger, African Americans developed a complex relationship to land, animals, and vegetation in American culture. Such poets as Terrance Hayes, Kendra Hamilton, and Jean Toomer speak of land turned and tilled by both forced and voluntary workers. One poet, Sean Hill, knows of such labor from his experience as a shepherd. Hill's poems are not the idylls of a city boy reflecting on the ease and peace and beauty of pastoral life. Life in the pasture was no lyre-accompanied romp for him. He worked hard and steadily, he witnessed grave injuries to humans and animals alike, and he regularly reckoned with death. His poem contrasts with the Romantics' pastoral imagery, which often portrayed the "noble savage" as a worker of the field, a shepherd or some other agrarian rube. As Wordsworth does in his poem "The Leech Gatherer," the poets of that influential period occupy positions of entitled privilege, observing the field worker but rarely actually working themselves. Whatever wisdom a lowly farmhand might convey must pass through an amanuensis's idealized observations of the wildness with which the worker communes. Such privilege of class, race, and station is interrogated by poems in this collection like Hill's "Seven Pastorals at Sixteen" and Yusef Komunyakaa's "Work." These poems prove what true wisdom can be conveyed when he who had been deemed savage or shepherd takes pen and tells his tale firsthand. Pets and prey, wild and tame, animal and vegetable, birds and insects included, the empathy and commiseration implicit in poems like Kwame Alexander's "Life," Audre Lorde's "The Bees," and Alice Dunbar-Nelson's "April Is on the Way" reveal the astonishing degree to which these African American poets and their subjects have aligned themselves with the natural world. The historical scope of *Black Nature* demonstrates the ways in which black poets were investigating the alignment between man and nature long before the popularity of contemporary ecopoetics was confirmed.

For a people who have been classified as entirely separate, as a subspecies or as a possession, the demands of empathy and the repercussions of a lack of empathy are all the more apparent. The limits of pathetic fallacy and dominion are tested in poems that address the folly of drawing analogies between our relationships with other creatures and the workings of the human heart. As the speaker in Carl Phillips's "White Dog" lets the animal go into the snow, he understands: "She seems a part of me, // and then she seems entirely like what she is: / a white dog." Releasing the dog "is not like wanting to learn what losing a thing we love feels like." The dog is no extension of the speaker, and what love and connection the speaker holds for and with her must be held with the knowledge that she is her own completely separate entity, free to remove herself from the speaker entirely, and not subject to human emotions. In this poem, as with many others in this collection, the limits of man's actual, emotional, and imaginative control over the natural world are clearly drawn. In "White Dog," Phillips indicates there can be no real dominion because there is no real connection between man and beast, and thus the poem's speaker is able to cede his control over the animal. Conversely, in Lenard D. Moore's cheekily titled "Postcard to an Ecologist," the lack of an empathetic connection between man and beast contributes to the speaker's *willingness* to exercise the violent privilege of dominion. The speaker feels free to kill the snake he finds on his grandmother's land because he resists the concept of interdependency that the poet consciously mocks in his title.

But what of poems like Kamilah Aisha Moon's "What a Snakehead Discovered in a Maryland Pond and a Poet in Corporate America Have in Common," which draws a direct correlation between the natural world and the life and mind of the poet? What of the work of poets like Jessie Redmon Fauset and George Marion McClellan who were writing under the direct influence of Romanticism, a movement that, for better and for worse, assumed natural images ought to be employed in poems when they are "called for by a particular Sentiment"?[1] The limits of dominion, empathetic metaphor, and pathetic fallacy are tested in this anthology at both extremes. Black culture in America has embraced signification: the play of the natural world against the multiple connotations of the words used to describe it. Elements of the environment simultaneously function as imaginative, literal, and figurative realities. For example, the "river" in Rita Dove's "Three Days of Forest, a River, Free" is more than a moving body of water. It is a biblical allusion, a historical reality, a geographical boundary, a legal boundary, a decoy, the center of emotional and personal change, an aspiration, a metaphor: all these things at once. When Melvin B. Tolson describes the reactions of a sea turtle struggling in the belly of a shark, the real and implied correlation between the behaviors of these animals and the habits of Homo sapiens is undeniable. Many of this collection's poets remind us of the danger or futility of drawing too close a connection between our emotional landscapes and the realities and responses of the natural world, but others comfortably, sometimes aggressively, remind us how our place in the ecological web implicates the black community and the human race at large in emotional, practical, and creative ways.

Black Nature spans the history of black poetry in America. Including Phillis Wheatley's "On Imagination," from the first book of poetry ever published by a black person living in the American colonies, these works are a representative sampling of poems from each major movement in black American poetics as well as the newer poetry of contemporary poets still in the process of publishing their own collections. For some of these poets, the poems collected here are considered a crucial part of their oeuvre; for others, this anthology creates a new way of thinking about their work. The broad representation of historical time frames means that the concerns of the poets in the collection vary, given the historical contexts in which their poems were created. Though some conduct their business with little conscious awareness of political or historical contexts, others are inextricably connected to these moments. You will witness the progress (and sometimes decline) of history in the very roots and sap of the writing. Some of the poems and prose—Michael Harper's "History as Apple Tree," Anne Spencer's "White Things," Natasha Trethewey's "Monument," and Alice Walker's "The Flowers" included—place human bodies right into the ground so fruit and flower, ant and tree tangle themselves in human history even as they continue on their own, unconcerned agendas. Via indirect and direct comparison, the authors in this collection draw correlations between what happens to the rest of Earth's communities and what might happen to our own.

Recognition of the connectivity with worlds beyond the human is revealed as a necessity of spiritual and physical survival. One reason for the importation of black people to the North American continent was the perception of the economic benefits of the West Africans' agricultural aptitude and ability to survive in the extreme climate and environment of the southern American colonies and states. Those bound into slavery needed to know how to cultivate crops for the market as well as crops for their own gardens or shelters. Knowing what, how, and when to grow and harvest meant survival. Were a slave to choose another mode of existence, to chance freedom, running away likely involved periods of time in the wild. Knowledge of which direction moss grew on a tree, of how to throw a dog off a scent trail, what berries were edible, how to make a poultice for a wound, and of how to recognize which snakes were harmful—and which only looked that way—could mean the difference between another hour in freedom or an encounter with sudden danger or certain death. These historical and cultural realities are reflected in this book. Thylias Moss's "Sweet Enough Ocean, Cotton," Mark McMorris's "Aphrodite of Economy," and excerpts from Albery Whitman's *Rape of Florida* are all examples of works that examine nature's historical role in supporting or discouraging their subjects' aspirations, occupations, and survival.

Even during the most difficult periods of African American history, the natural world held potential to be a source of refuge, sustenance, and uncompromised beauty. Skills like knowing how to render discarded animal parts into edible meals, understanding which part of the swamp could provide long-term shelter, how to turn peaches into brandy, how to stew sour, wormy crab apples into sweet, delicious treats were aspects of physical and spiritual communion with the land. Time outdoors has proved refreshing and stimulating to many of the speakers recorded here. Quite a few reveal a connection with the world that is strong and deep. Cyrus Cassells's "Down from the Houses of Magic" and James Weldon Johnson's "Deep in the Quiet Wood" are exuberant celebrations of pleasant encounters with the natural world. In "For Alice Walker (a summertime tanka)," June Jordan recalls walking in a grove of ancient trees "talking Congo / gender grief and ash." Jordan expresses a sense of being overwhelmed, saying, "It's all so huge." Walker replies only, "These sweet trees: This tree." As with this example, the speakers of many of the poems move beyond personal, cultural, and political struggles into spaces of deep appreciation, connection, healing, and peace.

Perhaps, according to Elizabeth Dodd, "African American writers have not embraced nature writing" in the same manner as the dominant culture because "the literary attempt to deflect attention away from human beings . . . might not be appealing for writers who already feel politically, economically, and socially marginalized."[2] This theory helps explain some of the differences in approach of certain poems in this collection. Wanda Coleman's "Beaches. Why I Don't Care for Them," G. E. Patterson's "The Natural World," and Nikki Giovanni's "for saundra" all suggest a distaste for or disconnection from wilderness spaces. Like many of the poems in this anthology, they take a critical look at the natural world. Such criticism does not equal dismissal but, instead, indicates caution. Understanding this caution is a step toward understanding (and perhaps challenging) the disinterest many black Americans assert toward rural and remote landscapes. Rather than creating an oppositional framework, these poems formulate *alternative* frameworks for poetry.

Constructed to accommodate culturally informed perspectives on American social and literary history, *Black Nature* provides a crucial tool for broadening our concept of what it means to write about nature. According to such poets as Ed Roberson, Richard Wright, and Stephanie Pruitt, there is no place in the land where one can idle inattentively or harbor romanticized views. Interactions with the natural world demand respectful, honest attention and vigilant care.

Amaud Jamal Johnson's "The Maple Remains" and Paul Laurence Dunbar's "The Haunted Oak" speak directly to some of the more disturbing roots of this justifiable concern. These poems portray the grisly function America's trees have served and the shame that hangs about a place long after an awful deed is done. Many of the poems in this collection point to the collusion between nature and man, the manner in which the natural world has been used to destroy, damage, or subjugate African Americans. Even those poets who write decades after and miles away from the locus of the events they describe reveal caution and heightened awareness. In his poem "Migration," Major Jackson writes: "I read oaks and poplars for signs: charred branches / Tobacco leaves strung up to die, swamp soil in my soul. / Ever trace the outline of a phantom mob, even if you were late arriving?" Given the active history of betrayal and danger in the outdoors, it is no wonder that many African Americans link their fears directly to the land that witnessed or abetted centuries of subjugation.

Even beyond the mediation of human activities, the natural world contains much that demands attention. Survival in hostile environments depends on understanding the very complexity of these environments. In a swamp, the terrain and the animal life might act as savior, whereas the introduction of human cultivation could threaten the shelter a runaway had found in the wild. Animals and plants that seem innocuous, like starlings (Robert Hayden), ladybugs (Amber Flora Thomas), or roses (June Jordan) are problematized in this anthology; on the other hand, creatures commonly viewed as nuisances, like the fox (C. S. Giscombe), the cockroach (Lucille Clifton), and the skunk (Marilyn Nelson), are esteemed. Poems like Harryette Mullen's "European Folk Tale Variant" and Janice Harrington's "O Believer" urge us to look carefully in order to correctly identify various loci of danger. The poems remind us that culturally informed fears, alignments, and memories run deeper than expected, and they can stem from unexpected sources.

Until the late nineteenth century, 90 percent of America's black population lived in the rural American South.[3] Now, at the start of the twenty-first century, the majority of America's black population lives in major urban centers. We often hear about the Great Migration of the late nineteenth and early twentieth centuries, population redistributions precipitated by difficulties claiming a stake in the land people worked, but, as Frank X Walker's "Homeopathic" and Ruth Ellen Kocher's "At 57, My Father Learns to Grow Things" remind us, it is important to note that, even in the face of massive urbanization, African Americans still received regular sustenance from a wide variety of plant and animal life. As access to education increased, and through the early 1970s, a significant percentage of African Americans received some or all of their secondary or higher education at state land-grant universities and agricultural and vocational technology institutions like Iowa State or Booker T. Washington's Tuskegee Institute. George Washington Carver, the subject of several poems in this collection, attended a number of these schools and ended his life and career at Tuskegee. Claude McKay left Tuskegee and "shoved off for Kansas State as a less mechanized agricultural science major, where he excelled in Advanced Grammar and allowed himself to fail in Stock Judging I."[4] Yusef Komunyakaa, the first (and thus far only) African American male to receive a Pulitzer Prize in poetry, earned his M.A. in creative writing from Colorado State University, the state's flagship agricultural university. Given this educational legacy, a fundamental aspect of the intellectual development of many African Americans, our poets included, is planted in the land, in the agrarian roots of this country.

Despite all these connections to America's soil, we don't see much African American poetry in nature-related anthologies because, regardless of their presence, blacks have not been recognized in their poetic attempts to affix themselves to the landscape. They haven't been seen, or when they have it is not as people who are rightful stewards of the land. They are accidentally or invisibly or dangerously or temporarily or inappropriately on/in the landscape. The majority of the works in this collection incorporate treatments of the natural world that are historicized or politicized and are expressed through the African American perspective, which inclines readers to consider these texts as political poems, historical poems, protest poems, socioeconomic commentary, anything but nature poems. This is particularly true when the definition of what constitutes literature about nature or the environment is limited to poems that address the pastoral or the wild, spaces and subjects removed or distanced from human contact. The alternative formulations and representations collected here are often not considered when anthologies, syllabi, and papers about nature or environmental literature are compiled. This collection provides evidence for their inclusion.

Poetry has been the medium through which an overwhelming number of African American literary figures first made their names, and poetry is a genre in which treatments of nature are expected. However, *Black Nature* is the first collection of American nature writing that focuses on poetry written by African Americans. If nature poetry is, as the introduction to the *Oxford Book of Nature Writing* suggests, "a history of our views about ourselves," why have African Americans been excluded?[5] Perhaps because of the history of oppression and hardship, coupled with the shift toward urbanization after the northern migrations, it was difficult for black and white Americans to evoke positive memories of and poems by African Americans in the natural world. Perhaps, as bell hooks suggests, "When black people migrated to urban cities, this humanizing connection with nature was severed. . . . When this thinking was coupled with a breakdown in religiosity, a refusal to recognize the sacred in everyday life, it served the interests of white supremacist capitalist patriarchy."[6] Despite the protestations inherent in the existence of the poems in this anthology, the propagated belief that black people have little or no creatively intellectual connection to the natural world perhaps serves some larger purpose in terms of an imaginative and exclusionary formulation of America. There are any number of explanations for the exclusion of black nature poetry from the dominant canon to date, but in its origins and in each of its major renaissances, black poetry in America has recorded perspectives on the natural world as various as black perspectives on the nation. A broader understanding of this country and its poetry is occluded when we overlook or refuse to look carefully at black poets' varied use of landscape, animal life, and ecological poetics. *Black Nature* documents this truth.

Every attempt has been made to secure permissions for a wide range of the most compelling poems on this subject. Poets are represented by a greater or lesser number of poems based partly on the frequency with which they write about these subjects as well as on the manner in which their work connects to the main themes chronicled in this collection. There are a few poets whose work a knowledgeable reader of African American poetry might consider an omission from this anthology. In most instances, the poets or their estates were contacted, but, unfortunately, reproduction rights could not be negotiated for this edition. Should a future edition of this collection appear, the opportunity to remedy these losses will surely be sought out. While acknowledging that the realities of the publishing world mean a certain few poets must necessarily be left out of this anthology, the comprehensive scope of this book is unique. The 93 poets and 180 poems assembled here represent the first and largest collection of African American nature poets and poetry ever published.

Because so many of the poems in this collection address nature in ways that challenge accepted notions about what qualifies as environmental or ecological poetry, ten introductory prose pieces provide frameworks to explain each of the anthology's cycles. Most of the prose pieces were composed by writers who are poets themselves. Their understanding of African American literary and cultural history and the specificity of African American poetics add to this collection's reexamination of the importance of these poems in the broader discussion of American literature and nature literature, and they position African American poetics within these contexts.

Given the scope and continuity of the selections in *Black Nature*, rather than organizing the collection in chronological order, I have established ten cycles that highlight recurrent concerns. The thematic organization of the collection helps readers to reconceptualize the boundaries for environmentally minded writing. While a number of the poems included in the anthology address standard topics of nature writing, others reimagine the boundaries of the genre, all working to remind readers that we are always part of the natural world, even when we feel most alienated from it. Some narrators revel in the world they see around them, while others take that world for granted or actively rebel against what they encounter. *Black Nature* tracks a phasic shift from connection to disaffection and back.

Cycle One, "Just Looking," establishes a framework through which we encounter African American poets recognizing the beauty and potential of open spaces. Lucille Clifton's "the earth is a living thing" reflects a cosmology of connectivity. Al Young's "The Mountains of California: Part I" and Robert Hayden's "Night Blooming Cereus" revel in the incredible beauty of the witnessed world. Even George Moses Horton, writing from slavery, is able to recognize the splendor of the landscape surrounding him. Some of the poets in this cycle, like Helene Johnson, complicate the scenes they describe by bringing in instances of change, violence, and even death. However, their observations are realistic renderings of the complex beauty they witness. In poems that consciously address the creative process, such poets as Alvin Aubert and Rachel Eliza Griffiths warn against reducing the realities of the natural world in an attempt to conform to a potentially vapid lyric landscape tradition. The poets in this cycle all suggest that they are not cowed by the magnitude of the natural world. They are able to appreciate nature on its own terms.

Cycle Two, "Nature, Be with Us," continues on the path set by the previous cycle, illuminating alignments between the human and natural world. In "To Waste at Trees," Gerald Barrax Sr. reminds readers that it is only when we begin to not "care about the world" that we "let them make us deceive ourselves / That seasons have no meaning for us." Some of the alignments portrayed in Cycle Two are tight bonds, some very loose, and throughout the cycle there are growing threats of potentially irrevocable rifts. However, even in urban centers (Ed Roberson), even after witnessing the destruction of Hurricane Katrina (Reginald Shepherd), while watching a woman garden (Sterling Brown), and speaking to an unborn child (Ross Gay), these poems stay grounded in the earth and connected to the varied and marvelous communities with which we cohabitate.

Cycle Three, "Dirt on Our Hands," investigates sources of alienation from or betrayal by the land. The alienation is self-inflicted as much as it is created by external circumstances such as slavery, tenant farming, and population shifts away from rural landscapes. In "Another April," Anne Spencer's old gardener is inside, separated from her beloved garden by a window that ought to be cleaned. As we progress through the cycle, the barriers that have been established between humans and the natural world grow more and more devastating, encouraging destruction and disaffection, discouraging cooperative thinking, and eventually ushering in certain trauma and death. In "Sorrow Home," Margaret Walker laments "the Klan of hate, the hounds and / the chain gangs keep me from my own." Though several of these poets resist this final outcome, even those who try to forge or re-forge a connection are thwarted.

Sometimes in the form of pests, sometimes pets, sometimes work animals, and sometimes wild, for better and for worse, the animals who share our spaces enforce humility by keeping us in touch with a world beyond the human. Poems in Cycle Four, "Pests, People Too," address power negotiations between humans, insects, and other troublesome creatures. These poems warn us that if a connection between the human world and others is severed, our lives will be more desperate still. Lucille Clifton suggests that the end of the world will be ushered in when cockroaches "bow their / sad heads for us not at us / and march single file away." Other poets in this section, directly and indirectly, draw a connection between African Americans and birds, insects, and other marginalized creatures. In Robert Hayden's "A Plague of Starlings," he describes the few starlings who return after a flock has been thinned:

> The spared return,
> when the guns are through,
> to the spoiled trees
> like choiceless poor
> to a dangerous
> dwelling place.

In the lot of these birds are echoes of the lot of the urban poor. Once the connection between the human experience and the experiences of other living creatures is severed, it becomes easier to destroy any form of life that appears to be in competition with our own.

As the anthology progresses, the apparent complicity of the natural world in the difficult circumstances of the poems' subjects increases. Cycle Five, "Forsaken of the Earth," opens with a poem by Phillis Wheatley in which she describes all the wonders her imagination can create. The poem ends with the poet's powers being stripped from her. She must remain silent because the climate of the slave society in which she finds herself "forbids" her aspirations. When she writes "Northern tempests damp the rising fire," Wheatley describes Boston's weather and its society, and their effects on the region, the hearth, and the heart. Written in terms simultaneously literal and figurative, personal and political, general and specific, this poem, like so many of the works in this collection, resists dichotomization. In this poem and others in Cycle Five, the line between the harm humans do to one another and that delivered by environmental forces blurs. These poems implicate the natural world in a personal or collective history of trauma. The plants, animals, water, and weather seem to be complicit with society, creating various taunts and tragedies even while flaunting potential beauty and possibility. As Cycle Five progresses, aspirations dwindle, and articulated more and more frequently are expressions of frustration or exasperation, descriptions of the natural forces that got the poems' subjects to this place of discontent.

Cycle Six, "Disasters, Natural and Other," continues in a similar vein, but culpability is more clearly drawn in this section than in the previous one. Whereas in the poems in Cycle Five the natural world might be marginally complicit in the harm done to African Americans, in the poems collected in Cycle Six the natural world is the direct cause of devastation. The subjects in these poems are abandoned to its fickle mercies. Sterling Brown's "Children of the Mississippi," Askia M. Touré's "Floodtide," and Ishmael Reed's "Earthquake Blues" all lay blame for disasters squarely upon natural forces. Douglas Kearney composed "Floodsong 2: Water Moccasin's Spiritual" by directly quoting, but also completely rearranging, the classic negro spiritual:

> trouble
> > in the water
> > > trouble
> > in the water
>
> > > water
> > > water
> > > water
> god's gon'

The sense of abandonment the subjects of these poems feel is profound, and their alienation is easily attributable to naturally provoked disasters. That said, it was compounded human neglect that allowed catastrophes like Hurricane Katrina and the other great floods along the Mississippi basin to cause as much destruction as they did. Some poems in Cycle Six, like Audre Lorde's "Song," Amber Flora Thomas's "Erasure," and Yusef Komunyakaa's "A Greenness Taller Than Gods," place human-provoked disasters within natural settings that encourage them. Throughout this cycle, in an array of circumstances, natural forces of devastation overwhelm the speakers of these poems.

Poets who think carefully about nature and African American life observe that forces separate from us, sometimes greater than us, continue to function alongside and often regardless of our agendas. Cycle Seven, "Talk of the Animals," contains a number of poems that look at the ways in which the animal world in particular operates separately from or in relationship to African Americans or humanity in general. The poems in this section situate humans in conversation with or about animals, illustrating ideas about intraspecies responsibilities, relationships, and responses. Wendy S. Walter's "Man Raised as Chicken," Cornelius Eady's "Speed," Shara McCallum's "The Spider Speaks," and Rachel Eliza Griffiths's "Black-and-White Dusk at Limantour Beach" prove that our concept of who we are is developed within the context of who and what surrounds us. The poems in Cycle Seven expand the boundaries of our communities to remind us that we exist in relationship to communities and environments much larger than ourselves.

The history of the land we spring from tells us much about ourselves, but for a community of people that has been continually displaced from or abused in the name of the land, these revelations are not always comforting. Poems in Cycle Eight, "What the Land Remembers," reveal the history stored in natural bodies. These poems echo much of the frustration and desperation illuminated in earlier cycles, and the poets here, writing primarily from the latter part of the twentieth century, do so with a well-developed historical consciousness. Placed within a historical and contemporary context of struggle, displacement, and search for security, poems like E. Ethelbert Miller's "I Am Black and the Trees Are Green" and C. S. Giscombe's "the future" were created from intersections of personal experience, collective history, and landscape. The natural tropes and landscapes in these poems reveal the legacy of slavery, the reign of terror visited by lynching and segregation, as well as the persistent belief of the poems' subjects in the potential for positive change.

As the twentieth century progressed, so did the freedoms of black Americans. The 1960s and 1970s ushered in a period of cultural reclamation and pride; the 1980s and 1990s brought an increase in economic access for many; the advent of the environmental justice movement at the end of the twentieth century drew attention to the link between the land and health, access, and opportunity. These circumstances encouraged black Americans to actively reclaim their stake in the natural world. Cycle Nine, "Growing Out of This Land," is the only group of poems to include entirely contemporary texts, all published after 1970. In the midst of canonical figures in African American letters like June Jordan and Audre Lorde, the work of such new talents as Gregory Pardlo, Remica Bingham, and Indigo Moor advances notions of African Americans' renewed connection with the land. These poets' reflections on the positive and negative effects of the personal and collective cultivation of ecological spaces reveal a new mode of thinking and writing about human interactions with the environment. Developing within the contemporary American landscape, these poets, many of whom were born after 1965 and thus the beneficiaries of gains from the Civil Rights and Black Power movements, create new ways to thrive within the natural realities of the world that surrounds them.

Cycle Ten, "Comes Always Spring," is a reblossoming of the connections forged in the previous cycle. Though many of these poets evoke histories of violence, devastation, or death, they see their own potential reflected in the world around them. Ross Gay suggests that if you should come to an understanding that "all you love will turn to dust," you should not fight this knowledge. Instead, "Walk through the garden's dormant splendor. / Say only, thank you." From similar realizations come a variety of epiphanies of connections and regenerations. Margaret Walker sees "Resurrection / over and over again" in "My Mississippi Spring," and in "The Man. His Bowl. His Raspberries," Claudia Rankine revels in the fact that, "gently, taking," her speaker "gets what he needs" from a bountiful raspberry bush. The cycle's last poem, in which Tim Seibles describes shoots of grass "rising in spite of every plot / against them," underscores the spirit in which the cycle, and this anthology, end. Despite the hardships visited upon African Americans and the natural world they live in, hope and potential for renewal, regeneration, and positive growth spring eternally.

Black Nature brings to light the myriad ways African American poets have engaged the conflicts and confluences between their environments and their daily lives. Its cycles encourage readers to divert their gaze into new directions, demanding they notice new aspects of the world and accept alternative modes of description. Some poems resemble traditional pastorals, in which speakers escape through landscape into spaces that allow unhindered imaginative freedom. In others, overland escapes promise, and sometimes fulfill, actual legal and physical freedom. The transformative powers of nature yield potential for facilitating change in the world. In many poems the landscape is tainted by a legacy of racially motivated brutality, while in others the promise of a future unfettered by fear is realized through the natural forces of change. People work in these poems, and they reflect and relax as well. They form alliances with plants and animals as often as they question those alliances. They look at trees and see history, many sources of horror. They look at trees and see grandeur, sources of sustenance, beauty, and shade.

NOTES

1. John Keats as quoted in John Felstiner, *Can Poetry Save the Earth? A Field Guide to Nature Poems* (New Haven: Yale University Press, 2009), 57.

2. Elizabeth Dodd, "The Great Rainbowed Swamp: History as Moral Ecology in the Poetry of Michael Harper," in *Beyond Nature Writing: Expanding the Boundaries of Ecocriticism*, ed. Karla Armbruster and Kathleen R. Wallace (Charlottesville: University Press of Virginia, 2001).

3. bell hooks, "Earthbound: On Solid Ground," in *The Colors of Nature: Culture, Identity, and the Natural World,* ed. Alison H. Deming and Lauret E. Savoy (Minneapolis: Milkweed Editions, 2002).

4. William J. Maxwell, ed., *Claude McKay: Complete Poems* (Urbana: University of Illinois Press, 2004).

5. Richard Mabey, ed., *The Oxford Book of Nature Writing* (New York: Oxford University Press, 1995).

6. bell hooks, "Earthbound: On Solid Ground," in *The Colors of Nature.*

CYCLE ONE

Just Looking

ED ROBERSON

We Must Be Careful

Writing poetry, for me, began with the nature poem. Most beginning writers record outpourings of their most personal emotions of adolescent conflict, usually love. I did that, but not so much as pouring out my feelings about what I was doing, which was traveling around Alaska, Canada, the United States, and Bermuda "doing nature." I was an undergraduate research assistant in limnology, freshwater chemistry, collecting samples in the field, recording and analyzing data on a very simple level. My first nationally published poem as grand prize winner in the *Atlantic Monthly* sounds like the god of nature's undergraduate lab assistant: "must be careful . . ."

By the end of this early poem, nature turns into words; the poem is as much about the experience of writing as it is about the experience and observation of nature. I think this poem is also my early understanding of words as appropriation, not just a simple picture of the unknown focused into the realm of the known.

Appropriation implies that, in the takeover, the taken object is changed to conform to the taker, to the carrier. Those are *my* words carrying *my* carefully chosen deer, my grizzlies, not Nature's. Like stuffing and mounting them on the wall, I appropriate the grizzlies without active appetites or teeth, for a quiet, nonlethal poem. The teeth stay behind in Nature. The missing appetite and teeth reinforce my sense that human experience of nature differs from Nature, that there is always an unknowable, hidden aspect of Nature.

This mystery beyond words is our mythology, our religion, our poetry. We exist in the midst of living as other living. We have words for our existence; but after enough words, we come to the limits of—if not our living—our knowledge of the nature of human living. There is, however, no humanly containable limit to living Nature; there is no outside of Nature.

In most ecopoetics, a poet's way of writing about nature, man can't be outside Nature; our life exists inside as an act of Nature. Even our experience of a supernatural arises as a likeness to this limitation, out of our being.

Today's ecologically conscious poet sees the world of human existence resting in, on, or arising, precipitating out of the Earth: out of all life, out of Nature. The nature poem occurs when an individual's sense of the larger Earth enters into the world of human knowledge. The main understanding that results from this encounter is *the* Ecopoetic: that the world's desires do *not* run the Earth, but the Earth *does* run the world.

The Earth, or Nature, is very generous with this datum. The lines from "must be careful . . ." came out of a job located geographically in Alaska, but come first from a place where the unknown, uncontrollable aspects of bears and mountains step around the word *Alaska* to locate me in the barely mapped nature of Earth.

Ever since Alaska, I've been "doing nature"; taking down the data in my writing, not only of the present natural world but the data on myself in that world, on myself as just another one of nature's innumerable components. This self-conscious attention to being in balance—careful, to being a part of nature, not separate as its master or its crown—was to become one of the basic positions of my ecopoetics. My orderly handling of the nature poem came from my feel for basic scientific observation and technique, not the order of a metaphysical imperative. Not even a green peace.

I had been at the mercy of nature's "fragrant innocence" in the Upper Amazon jungle and climbing in the Andes Mountains; and the "green Thought in a green Shade" had been an actual jaguar probably seeing me with the thought of dinner. Off the page, Marvell's garden feeds both ways. My place in nature could be to feed an animal life as well as to be fed the nectarine and peach of Marvell's poem. This leveling fear exposed another difference between my experience and nature poetry. Against the eternal idyll of Romantic nature, I had to place the idea of subjective limit, of de-centered mortality. . . .

A traditional *gomby*, or stilt walker, prays or chants himself out of his body into "spirit," a state of possession that lifts him onto his stilts. To see the gomby, they appear to be flying bodies above the crowd; their legs stretched by the lift-off just barely still touch the ground. In one of my poems, the gomby has the spirit of a heron, and I am the fish he is hunting. I am one of the prey of Earth; here, not to be eaten, but rather made to see my human world through eyes located elsewhere in the Earth/Nature. I am not made to see death, but rather to see what it is to almost instinctively turn and face knowledge beyond my current grasp. To be "possessed," en-tranced by Earth.

Jonathan Bate says it is "the capacity of the writer to restore us to the earth which is our home." Nature is not a caring mother addressed solely to our needs; the Earth has no perception of us as we see ourselves and our needs. "The initial relationship between humanity and environment is in relationships of utility and potential resource." Technology is more likely to "conserve, regenerate and nourish the resource base of capitalism" than nature. Africans who came enslaved to this country as a commercially exploitable resource experienced how the parallels in policies of colonialism and the one-sided exploitation of natural ecologies deform human relationships. But Africans also brought a relationship to Nature with them that defended them against this distortion. "High John the Conquer (conjure) Root" is a spirit plant you can eat and use to cure, but you had to know what to look for to find him. This is not so much anthropomorphizing of Nature as it is an observant accumulating of the knowledge of self in an also living environment.

At its base, like that African retention, Bate's idea of the need to be "restored to the earth" is to offset the developed alienation that comes with those commercial kinds of relationships, of exploitation we experience. In my own poems I try to show our social nature in and as the growth of our cities and city culture. Our technology, however, is more likely to conserve, regenerate, and nourish the limiting and exclusive resource base of capitalism than our larger human or Earth/Nature. Restoring this larger Earth to urban poetry, embedding city life within a living Nature focuses on an interrelation that should keep us sensitized to exploitative relationships which could cut us off, cut us out of life. In an African sense, extinction also is a spirit plant that probably grows where HighJohn the Conjaroot grows, and we have to know what we're looking for . . . or we'll find him. Can you O.D. on life? Maybe that's a whole new aspect of urban nature poetry that needs to be written.

the earth is a living thing

is a black shambling bear
ruffling its wild back and tossing
mountains into the sea

is a black hawk circling
the burying ground circling the bones
picked clean and discarded

is a fish black blind in the belly of water
is a diamond blind in the black belly of coal

is a black and living thing
is a favorite child
of the universe
feel her rolling her hand
in its kinky hair
feel her brushing it clean

The Mountains of California: Part I

These demonstrations of the one God,
green in the springtime in wintertime too
& all that time John Muir was out here
                living with them,
breaking himself in on them,
I just ride amongst them inside a car,
flip the radio off out of respect
& out of the feeling that there are
                more important waves
floating in & out of us, mostly thru us

The mountains of California,
do I have to say anything?
I love all this evidence
set up to surround me this way,
mountain, ocean, you just name it.

The Mountain Road Ends Here

When we are already giddy, the snow melts
and runs over the stones in the riverbed,
quickening our desire to return. This year
the small pink and blue alpine lupines pop up
before we get there. The July sun moves right
overhead, partly eclipsed by silhouettes
of birds we can't name.
                            The first marmot calls out
loudly to its cousins that we are coming,
and they scurry back to their burrows. Again,
we choose the flattest large rock on the ridge
for our picnic. Every year on our birthdays,
we eat artichokes, grilled mushrooms and olives,
here, on the side of the mountain where the light
lingers. The evergreens are slightly taller
than elsewhere though the cold keeps them small, holds them
close to the ground. Winter is at least a month
away from now. And here, we lie on our backs,
neither eating nor talking, watching the sky.

Queen Anne's Lace

Unseemly as a marvelous an astral renegade
now luminous and startling (rakish)
at the top of its thin/ordinary stem
the flower overpowers or outstares me
as I walk by thinking *weeds* and *poison
ivy, bush* and *fern* or *runaway grass:*
You (where are you, really?) never leave me
to my boredom: numb as I might like to be.
Repeatedly
you do revive
arouse alive

a suffering.

On Summer

Esteville fire begins to burn;
The auburn fields of harvest rise;
The torrid flames again return,
And thunders roll along the skies.

Perspiring Cancer lifts his head,
And roars terrific from on high;
Whose voice the timid creatures dread,
From which they strive with awe to fly.

The night-hawk ventures from his cell,
And starts his note in evening air;
He feels the heat his bosom swell,
Which drives away the gloom of fear.

Thou noisy insect, start thy drum;
Rise lamp-like bugs to light the train;
And bid sweet Philomela come,
And sound in front the nightly strain.

The bee begins her ceaseless hum,
And doth with sweet exertions rise;
And with delight she stores her comb,
And well her rising stock supplies.

Let sportive children well beware,
While sprightly frisking o'er the green;
And carefully avoid the snare,
Which lurks beneath the smiling scene.

The mistress bird assumes her nest,
And broods in silence on the tree,
Her note to cease, her wings at rest,
She patient waits her young to see.

The farmer hastens from the heat;
The weary plough-horse droops his head;
The cattle all at noon retreat,
And ruminate beneath the shade.

The burdened ox with dauntless rage,
Flies heedless to the liquid flood,
From which he quaffs, devoid of gauge,
Regardless of his driver's rod.

Pomaceous orchards now expand
Their laden branches o'er the lea;
And with their bounty fill the land,
While plenty smiles on every tree.

On fertile borders, near the stream,
Now gaze with pleasure and delight;
See loaded vines with melons teem—
'Tis paradise to human sight.

With rapture view the smiling fields,
Adorn the mountain and the plain,
Each, on the eve of Autumn, yields
A large supply of golden grain.

The Yellow Jacket

We pause in our day
Before completion of evening
Chores
I to cook dinner
And you . . . I'm not sure
What you do

I empty the birdbaths
Always worrying
A virus or germ
Or unpleasant bacteria may lurk
To do fatal harm
To those who only bring
Their voices in joy
And thanksgiving for fresh water

And you buzz and . . . quite frankly . . . annoy
Me as I go about this duty
Fulfilling a contract that was
Never signed and is not at all
Enforceable
But nonetheless a cheerful
Duty to our feathered friends

Recognizing each tree gone
Each bush removed for a deck
Or a patio has left a place
Less welcoming I hope
The birds accept this clean water
As a suitable replacement

I swat at you worried
You will sting
Causing my throat to swell
Blocking my air or
Some other unknown danger
Humans attribute when we hear
Buzzes

You wait . . . buzz by . . .
And wait again
Until the water is filled
Where you can sit
Majestically on the edge
And drink

We are not friends
The yellow jacket and I
You will not be tamed
Or trained
Your sound will offer no comfort
Nor your numbers any sense
Of safety

Yet in this evening
Watching you drink
I am in awe
Of your self-possessed
Beauty

Eclogue at Twilight

The three wrestle in the grass
five or ten minutes, shaking blooms
& winged seeds to the ground.
The lioness lays a heavy paw on the jackal's chest,
almost motherly. His mate
backs off a few yards. Eyeball
to eyeball, they face each other
before she bites into his belly
& tugs out the ropy entrails
like loops of wet gauze.
Time stops. She'd moved
through the tall yellow sage
as they copulated,
stood only a few feet
away, enveloped in the scent
that drew them together.
When they first saw her
there, they couldn't stop.
Is this how panic & cunning
seethe into the bloodstream?
Without the power to forgive,
locked in ritual, the fight
began before they uncoupled.
A vulture, out of the frame,
draws an unbroken spiral
against the plains & sky.
Black quills scribble
slow as the swing of a hypnotist's
gold chain. For a moment, it seems
she's snuggling up to the jackal.

Maybe the wild aroma of sex
plagues the yellow grass.
A drizzle adds its music
to the background,
& a chorus of young girls
chants from across the hills.
For a man who stumbles
on this scene, with Hegel
& awe in his head, he can't
say if his mouth is opened
by the same cry & song.

Ruellia Noctiflora

A colored man come running at me out of the woods
last Sunday morning.
The junior choir was going to be singing
at Primitive Baptist over in Notasulga,
and we were meeting early to practice.
I remember wishing I was barefoot
in the heavy, cool-looking dew.
And suddenly this tall, rawbone wild man
come puffing out of the woods, shouting
Come see! Come see!
Seemed like my mary janes just stuck
to the gravel. Girl, my heart
like to abandon ship!

Then I saw by the long tin cylinder
slung over his shoulder on a leather strap
and his hoboish tweed jacket
and the flower in his lapel
that it was the Professor.
He said, gesturing,
his tan eyes a blazing,
that last night,
walking in the full moon light,
he'd stumbled on
a very rare specimen:
Ruellia noctiflora,
the night-blooming wild petunia.
Said he suddenly sensed a fragrance
and a small white glistening.

It was clearly a petunia:
The yellow future beckoned   *"future"*
from the lip of each tubular flower,
a blaring star of frilly, tongue-like petals.
He'd never seen this species before.
As he tried to place it,
its flowers gaped wider,
catching the moonlight,
suffusing the night with its scent.   *"suffusing*
All night he watched it   *gradually spread*
promise silent ecstasy to moths.   *through or over*
                    connection to
                          nature

If we hurried, I could see it
before it closed to contemplate
becoming seed.
Hand in hand, we entered
the light-spattered morning-dark woods.
Where he pointed was only a white flower
until I saw him seeing it.

Evening Primrose

Poetically speaking, growing up is mediocrity.
—Ned Rorem

Neither rosy nor prim,
not cousin to the cowslip
nor the extravagant fuchsia—
I doubt anyone has ever
picked one for show,
though the woods must be fringed
with their lemony effusions.

Sun blathers its baronial
endorsement, but they refuse
to join the ranks. Summer
brings them in armfuls,
yet, when the day is large,
you won't see them fluttering
the length of the road.

They'll wait until the world's
tucked in and the sky's
one ceaseless shimmer—then
lift their saturated eyelids
and blaze, blaze
all night long
for no one.

The Night-Blooming Cereus

     And so for nights
we waited, hoping to see
the heavy bud
       break into flower.

     On its neck-like tube
hooking down from the edge
of the leaf-branch
       nearly to the floor,

     the bud packed
tight with its miracle swayed
stiffly on breaths
       of air, moved

     as though impelled
by stirrings within itself.
It repelled as much
       as it fascinated me

     sometimes—snake,
eyeless bird head,
beak that would gape
       with grotesque life-squawk.

     But you, my dear,
conceded less to the bizarre
than to the imminence
       of bloom. Yet we agreed

we ought
to celebrate the blossom,
paint ourselves, dance
in honor of

archaic mysteries
when it appeared. Meanwhile
we waited, aware
of rigorous design.

Backster's
polygraph, I thought,
would have shown
(as clearly as it had

a philodendron's
fear) tribal sentience
in the cactus, focused
energy of will.

The belling of
tropic perfume—that
signaling
not meant for us;

the darkness
cloying with summoning
fragrance. We dropped
trivial tasks

and marveling
beheld at last the achieved
flower. Its moonlight
petals were

            still unfold-
ing, the spike fringe of the outer
perianth recessing
            as we watched.

            Lunar presence,
foredoomed, already dying,
it charged the room
            with plangency → *loud, reverberating often melancholy*

            older than human
cries, ancient as prayers
invoking Osiris, Krishna,
            Tezcátlipóca.

            We spoke
in whispers when   *lack of voice*
we spoke   *& platform*
            at all . . .

GEORGE MARION McCLELLAN

A September Night

Anguilla, Mississippi, September, 1852

The full September moon sheds floods of light,
And all the bayou's face is gemmed with stars
Save where are dropped fantastic shadows down
From sycamores and moss-hung cypress trees.
With slumberous sound the waters half asleep
Creep on and on their way, 'twixt rankish reeds,
Through marsh and lowlands stretching to the gulf.
Begirt with cotton-fields Anguilla sits
Half bird-like dreaming on her summer nest
Amid her spreading figs and roses still
In bloom with all their spring and summer hues.
Pomegranates hang with dapple cheeks full ripe,
And over all the town a dreamy haze
Drops down. The great plantations stretching far
Away are plains of cotton downy white.
Oh, glorious is this night of joyous sounds
Too full for sleep. Aromas wild and sweet,
From muscadine, late-blooming jessamine,
And roses, all the heavy air suffuse.
Faint bellows from the alligators come
From swamps afar, where sluggish lagoons give
To them a peaceful home. The katydids
Make ceaseless cries. Ten thousand insects' wings
Stir in the moonlight haze, and joyous shouts
Of Negro song and mirth awake hard by
The cabin dance. Oh, glorious is the night.
The summer sweetness fills my heart with songs
I cannot sing, with loves I cannot speak.

THYLIAS MOSS

Sweet Enough Ocean, Cotton

I haven't seen the sea before
but it must be easy to love

because even without ever seeing it before
I call the blown-open cotton a sea,
I call moving through the rows
my attempt to walk on rough water.

It's not that the cotton seems watery
or that each cotton seed hair is like
a separate one of the sparkles the sun makes
when its light bounces in moving water,

—though it is like that
now that I think about it.

It's just how big
the cotton is. This small field

seems bigger than the sky,
and is the sky for ants. It's just

how the cotton carries you,
delivers you on a rocky shore,
shipwrecks you,

strands you

even though you can't argue
against what good it does

because you have been taken up in
the persuasion of a garment, of a cocoon.

I've been thinking about this.
While I'm working, I think
about this. My mind is the part of me
that gets the least rest.

It's never quiet;
there's always the hum
inside me, the hive free inside me
making me think about honey, dipping
all my thoughts into honey

and even the thoughts honey won't
stick to have been in the honey,
have been next to honey so the knowledge
of honey is on them and the knowledge
all by itself can be sweet enough.

I think about that, think how thinking
can be sweet enough
forced compliance, thinking future
for now. Thinking about, thinking about
so much that is buried in the cotton.

Few months after we planted it,
I called the pink blooms of cotton before it ripened
an assault of endless sunset on the ocean.

"assault"

Metamorphism

Is this the sea?
This calm emotionless bosom,
Serene as the heart of a converted Magdalene—
Or this?
This lisping, lulling murmur of soft waters
Kissing a white beached shore with tremulous lips;
Blue rivulets of sky gurgling deliciously
O'er pale smooth-stones—
This too?
This sudden birth of unrestrained splendor,
Tugging with turbulent force at Neptune's leash;
This passionate abandon,
This strange tempestuous soliloquy of Nature,
All these—the sea?

a brown girl's nature poem: provincetown

a 'round the way girl says hey boys, i got a beach chair   i got
   yogurt   the sun on me
and south to bring   i won't even take a rock home   i learn seabird
   names
watch the 10 minute film about the glacier goin' back and forth big   over
   fifteen
thousand years   dig my feet in the latest deposit   and abandon
   making rules   just
listen as the glassy atlantic talks them   in her clear, bright voice

What More?

My lawnmower has awakened the resident god of my yard
who rubs its leafy hand in anticipation
of troubling me again with one of its cruel koans,

this one a small bird dropped
from the sky, or thrown out,
out of the sweetgum tree

where I was cutting
that long triangle of grass outside
the back fence: put there

when I wasn't looking, it lies
on its back twitching half in and out of the swath
I cut a minute before.

I'm being tampered with again,
like an electron whose orbit and momentum
are displaced by the scientist's measurement

and observation. If I'd found something already stiff
and cold on the ground
I'd have kicked or nudged it out of my path:

but the just-dead, the thing still warm,
just taken its last breath, made its last
movement, has its own kind of horror.

I leave the small patch of uncut grass around it.
Back inside my enclosed yard
I see a brown thrasher come and stand over the body,

with some kind of food in its bill.
(I was careful to say "bill" and not "mouth.")
By the next time I cut myself around the yard,

I see the thrasher sitting on the fence above the still dead,
still holding whatever it has in its bill. I've described
it all accurately. What more could anyone expect of me?

ED ROBERSON

be careful

i must be careful about such things as these.
the thin-grained oak.   the quiet grizzlies scared
into the hills by the constant tracks squeezing
in behind them closer in the snow.   the snared
rigidity of the winter lake.   deer after deer
crossing on the spines of fish who look up and stare
with their eyes pressed to the ice.   in a sleep.   hearing
the thin taps leading away to collapse like the bear
in the high quiet.   i must be careful not to shake
anything in too wild an elation.   not to jar
the fragile mountains against the paper far-   ⟶ *wrinkle* paper ?
ness.   nor avalanche the fog or the eagle from the air.
of the gentle wilderness i must set the precarious
words.   like rocks.   without one snowcapped mistake

Watching Blackbirds Turn to Ghosts

Tomoko and I talk a long time
about the gestures of a falling
leaf in autumn.

On the antenna outside
I watch a cloister of blackbirds
who are so still

they become the very shadows of blackbirds.

"The falling leaf is universal," she says
at one point.

We keep the leaf and its archetype
suspended in the air a bit longer
by talking slowly, in wonder,

while admitting it's consistently useless for us
to pretend to be clever in our poems.

I think of any leaf's shadow

going calmly to the street, beyond
the street, beyond the syntax of rot.

This morning I'd seen a woman
twisted like paper
at the bottom of a long bridge.

"Everyone will always watch leaves
fall in fall. Everyone will know this—
what it means—the simplicity

of the fall . . ."

ALVIN AUBERT

If Winter Comes, Can Spring?

in memory of western new york

one could say, simply, everything,
everywhere, is white. but that
would strain the point.
one might just as well declare
affirmative action. instead,
one observes, only, that there are
snow banks still that, despite
the negligible precipitation of
recent weeks, continue to grow,
mounting their stark precipices,
in the mind. mountains, and where
we are allowed to move at all
(one avoids saying "cliffs"), walls
of snow. deep white alleyways,
archeological in their alternate,
street plough shared layers of
dark and light dark and light,
of virginal snow and interim grime.
and solidifying all, the cold,
all movement whitely predetermined
and spring's inevitable advent
of minimal consolation.

EVIE SHOCKLEY

*31 words * prose poems*

[#12]

highly visual rural winter image seeks lyric poem (14–30 lines) for mutual enrichment and long-term relationship. image offers frostbitten river and fog-covered fields where snow seems to rise toward its origins.

Nature, Be with Us

We Are Not Strangers Here

A young black boy in Detroit, miles away from the nearest sea, dreamed of visiting underwater worlds. *Without leaving the room,* he recalled, *I would visit worlds I could hardly fathom.* When the young man reached adulthood, he sought out the natural world he had imagined as a child. The journey went beyond adventure and fantasy, because of the historical connection he found under the sea. He and a group of black scuba divers began to explore the wreckage of the slave ship *Henrietta Marie.* Exploring the sunken slaver was a bittersweet voyage but also a study in connectedness. The diver and journalist, Michael Cottman, shared the story of his connection to the natural world in his memoir *Spirit Dive.* A Detroit living room was miles away from the seas—their beauty and their tragedy—but the waters had been with him all along. He was not a stranger. His journey and his words tell us that we are not foreigners in the natural world.

I was drawn to Cottman's experience because it seems that many of us are spirit divers. We have immersed ourselves not just in the American outdoors, but we have also explored the emotional depths of the historical moments within nature. Waves of paradise waters carried slave ships. In southern woodlands grew both emancipation oaks and hanging trees. (Could some have been both? Can we ever know?) Along with the rice, tobacco, and cotton, the enslaved grew okra and yams, pieces of home for many transplanted Africans. The connections to nature, those that haunt and those that nurture, have been with us all along.

At some point, the terms *urban* and *black* became interchangeable. Such terminology would have us believe that our history began in cities and that we are a people of concrete and bricks, far removed from the oaks, rivers, and low country. But the black poets on these pages have illuminated the connections and their meanings across the generations.

Perhaps the affinity for nature was one of the few things the enslaved could carry with them, the contraband of the contraband. Although slaves were forced to become fixtures in the fields of the manmade American landscape, they were still patrons of the nature-made America—old-growth woods, littorals, and savannahs.

Like the spirit divers, black poets have long immersed themselves in moments of nature and then rendered those scenes on the page. The ebbs and flows of nature seem to guide the lines. There is the gentle flow of the wind and sea, but there are also other currents, historical and political, that are translated into language.

These words have helped to bridge the distance between an urbanized view of blackness and the natural world, a gap that, left unchecked, leaves more room for distortions. In his narrative, Cottman wrote of visiting the slave fortress on Gorée Island. He described an encounter with an American oilman staying at his hotel. The oilman felt it necessary to tell Cottman that Africans sold their own, *"You all did it to yourselves, too, you know,"* said the oilman to the diver, as if Europeans and Africans were somehow equal partners in the slave trade.

Thankfully, the spirit diver had already reclaimed his bridge to the natural world. He had explored waters and seen the shackles eaten away by the salt. He let nature tell its own truth, and perhaps he understood that we must be present to hear it.

If we are absent, then history will be written by the oilmen of the world, cultural mercantilists who extract resources and truths and rearrange them for their own purposes. What they extract is gone forever, leaving the landscape permanently altered.

As the poet explores nature, the extraction is much different. The takeaway is experiential, leaving the natural place intact for others who will come after. Instead of editing nature and the history therein, poets modify and rearrange nature on the page. This collection has gathered voices to present landscapes on the page. The very word *anthology* is rooted in nature. Bouquet. Garland. A harvest of language and imagery.

A young boy sat in a room and ventured to worlds unknown. As an adult, he affirmed that connection and spread it across his pages so it can be shared. The poems found herein reflect the ebbs, flows, and cycles of nature. They reflect a black experience no longer extracted or eroded, but renewed.

For a Farmer

Something slow moves through him, watched by hills.
Something low within each rock receives
His noonday wish, then crumbles rich; so fills
Each furrow that the prairie year upheaves.
His arm has lain with boulders. His copper hand
Has mused on roots, uncaring of barbed wire.
His fist has closed on thistle, and dug the land
For corn October snows have whelmed entire.
Something flows with him in stubborn streams,
And in the parted foliage something lives
In upright green, stirred by the rhythmic gleams
Of his hoe and spade. From worn-out arms he gives;
The earth receives, turns all his pain to soil,
Where he believes, and testifies through toil.

To Waste at Trees

Black men building a Nation,
My Brother said, have no leisure like them
No right to waste at trees
Inventing names for wrens and weeds.
But it's when you don't care about the world
That you begin owning and destroying it
Like them.

And how can you build
Especially a Nation
Without a soul?
He forgot that we've built one already—
In the cane, in the rice and cotton fields
And unlike them, came out humanly whole
Because our fathers, being African,
Saw the sun and moon as God's right and left eye,
Named Him Rain Maker and welcomed the blessings of his spit,
Found in the rocks his stoney footprints,
Heard him traveling the sky on the wind
And speaking in the thunder
That would trumpet in the soul of the slave.

Forget this and let them make us deceive ourselves
That seasons have no meanings for us
And like them
We are slaves again.

White Dog

First snow—I release her into it—
I know, released, she won't come back.
This is different from letting what,

already, we count as lost go. It is nothing
like that. Also, it is not like wanting to learn what
losing a thing we love feels like. Oh yes:

I love her.
Released, she seems for a moment as if
some part of me that, almost,

I wouldn't mind
understanding better, is that
not love? She seems a part of me,

and then she seems entirely like what she is:
a white dog,
less white suddenly, against the snow,

who won't come back. I know that; and, knowing it,
I release her. It's as if I release her
because I know.

you must walk this lonesome

say hello to moon leads you into trees as thick as folk on easter pews dark
but venture through amazing was blind but now fireflies glittering dangling
from evergreens like Christmas oracles soon you meet the riverbank down
by the riverside water bapteases your feet moon bursts back in low yellow
swing low sweet chariot of cheese shines on in the river cup hands and sip
what never saw inside a peace be still mix in your tears moon distills distress
like yours so nobody knows the trouble it causes pull up a log and sit until
your empty is full your straight is wool your death is yule moonshine will do
that barter with you what you got for what you need draw from the river like
it is well with my soul o moon you croon and home you go

Down from the Houses of Magic

1

Now the moon darns the moor with its fabric of minnows,
And the sea rushes with the ecstasy of ants.
Down from the houses of magic, a healing wind sweeps,
Down from the houses of magic.
On Gull Hill, in the flaming garden, God flings
A fistful of robin redbreasts—razzamatazz.
And the reed of the supple mind bends and shivers,
And the choirlike, match-stemmed, fiercely gallant flowers:
Johnny-jump-up, pert buttercup, anemone, peony, lupine,
The first lightning-white rose dying to open
Beneath the systole and diastole of a starry night,
Iris, allium, the proffered chalices of tulips,
The colors of a fabulous dusk in Tunisia;
Coming soon, a pleasure of freesias, a pleasure.
Such tintinnabulation—listen:
All the prayer-wheels of April-into-May luster
Spinning God-drunk—till finally beside
The moon-daft willow, slack as a marionette,
The frenzy of scotch broom,
The fleet-souled orioles marshal, at wolf's hour,
Then sally in one brilliant will.

2

Abundance begins here—at the sea lip:
On the Cape I've come to God and Proteus, come to rest in wild places:
Whisker-still galaxies of marshlands,
Beaches where I pause and study
The Atlantic, teal and taciturn, the Atlantic, glittering and fluent,

As on blond days fishermen stagger
And bluefish wake to the breathless dream of land.

Having combed eerie dunes,
I have been on desolate moons, wind-worked to pure scrimshaw,
And found deer, cranberries, a plum dusk,
Pools of sweet water carved into sand.

The streets stink of fish, after the dark
Gimcrack shawls of squalls and rain.
I amble through rumours of shipwrecks, ghosts,
Sense the red broom-sweep of the beacon even in my sleep—

I have my tremendous window.
The moon-jacklit boat comes to it, shimmering,
And the bride-sweet cirrus cloud,
And sometimes the streak of a squirrel, like the deft, sudden
Stroke of the watercolorist, whose brush distills the bay.

And now, clear and fugitive, in jack-in-the box brilliance,
The baby whale blooms:
Wild world, wild messenger—you are the moment's crown, sea-loved:
When providence brims to the outermost land,
No lack, no lack, but in my human mind.

3
Midsummer.
And after belligerent sun, twilight brings
A muezzin of sea-wind,
And the soul of the garden bows,
A praise in the earth:
Among Turk-cap lilies, suddenly,
In the willow's cool hair,
The breath of God—

Now I stand in the garden
Like a messenger proclaiming
I am Cyrus, and I am here,

Amid Lilliputian canon-flowers—
I surrender! I surrender!—
Under starry dippers pouring
Into a vast and holy dark—

4
One day on Gull Hill I wept and prayed:
Let this earth become a heaven—

Beyond the garden, the wall of clematis:
The world with its rills of blood,
The blue and virulent cell where a man was flayed
To make a flag of human skin—

Tonight the moon makes a silver threshing floor of the sea.
Beside the moth-claimed path, the stone seraph decays,
The stiffened body of a finch—

The rose is no paraclete.
A keen star plummets into the heart's cup, the summer grasses.

And the blue earth resumes its measureless dialogue
Between catastrophe and plenty.

5
The dirty, nail-bitten hand
Of a Black Lear,
With the green and pink
Bracelet of a woman,
Inching its way
Through garbage:

Even in the garden on Gull Hill,
I see that hand:
All day rocking back and forth
Between Turk-cap lilies and the trash—
Till at last words spill out,
Ones I shrink from:

Are you hungry all the time?

Yes, all the time—

O grant us strength to fashion a table
Where each of us has a name—

6
From autumn to autumn, teach us
How to breathe, endure,
In the shadow of the sickening weapon;

Teach us how to blossom,
If the sky is acid,
The garden marred—

We move through the world with its drastic reds,
Its discord,
Seeking balm in all things:
Mother's milk, the dream of reunion—

Not enough to hate suffering,
Hate war,
But to jettison at last
All duality, division,
To discern
God-in-the-guise-of-the-stranger,
God-in-the-guise-of-this-flesh—

7
Then in my dream, like a hawk,
I circled the garden:
No, it was not Earth, the grand, lacerated Earth;
On its whorled surface,
All the ages of humankind.

And a voice sang:
Here are flowers of deep suffering,
Swaying in the heart of God—

8

Because

   Each of us must seek
A finer life, a finer death.

Because

   In the garden, beside the clematis,
Jousting with slippery shadows
Of birth-and-death-and-birth-and-death,
Sometimes I come back to
The pitiless floor of Hiroshima,
Knowing in the terror and magnitude
Of true comprehension
I meant to die there—
Back to the fierce moment
After the *pika*, the flash,
When suddenly I reclaimed
A small, clear
Flicker of self—
My flesh gone,
But my soul still singing,
Adamant to live:

The history of survival is written under my lids.

9

And if the husk of the world is ripped away,

We will not have altered the consciousness of one leaf—

10

Let this earth become a heaven:
From the point of light within the mind of God,
The Earth hurling its roughhouse wills and lusters,

The Earth accruing poison—
Planet of joy, planet of crucifixion,
Piñata destined to be smashed—
Ashes, ashes,
All the mirrors of heaven blackening, imagine:
No lack, no lack, but in our human minds—

Let the clematis become a prayer
As clouds and canon-flowers ready
Sweet unguents of pollen and rain,
As God bellows, and a wild cavalry of wind sweeps
Down from the houses of magic
Down from the houses of magic
Down from the houses of magic

The Ephemera

Creatures of gauze and velvet wings.
    With life for one brief day,
Dancing and flitting where the breezes fling
    The sweets of blooming May;
Skimming the stream where the wild thyme grows,
    You dart with keen delight,
Only to die when the sweet wild rose
    Gives perfume to the night.

Weary at last, when the day is done,
    Of the breeze and clover's breath,
Folding your delicate wings with the sun,
    You gently drop to death;
Glimmering wings and a few short hours
    Were yours in sweet delight,
Living for a day in the world of flowers,
    And then—everlasting night.

Creatures of gauze and velvet wings,
    With a day of gleams and flowers,
Who knows—in the light of eternal things—
    Your life is less than ours?
Weary at last, it is ours, like you,
    When our brief day is done,
Folding our hands, to say adieu,
    And pass with the setting sun.

RUTH ELLEN KOCHER

Sleepwalker on the Mountain

> *And I search among the signs*
> *For the flare, polestar, pulley toward the edge.*
> —Ruth Stone

Half back to consciousness
she begins her nocturnal, locked-eye search
for the same torment that lives in trees,
arms outstretched as if the route
were more apparent in the dark,
the mountain like her country
shivering its hulk of plenty.
She hears leaves begging for warmth,
finds her coldness, her surprised feet,
and the barrenness comes easily as trouble.
She is the plight of winter trees,
the screech of their thrown branches
scraping windows, the misery of driftwood
searching for a boulder,
and though the wind tries to make all things equal
the sleeper's hands pierce air,
reaching to have the curses of wood,
of mountain dirt, of trees.
Somehow in sleep
she envies the oak stump in her path,
vacant of sap and chilled to its memory
of root; the broken trunk
sits high on a hill of maple,
loneliest of things.

RICHARD WRIGHT

#543

> "Let's make a scarecrow!"
> But after we made it,
>   Our field grew smaller.

Aphrodite of Economy

Landscape, as the events of a prior discontinuity,
will never know what we make of it, although
telegrams come, and breath hurries, at the top of a rise
to survey the orderly valleys, the young plantings
and the mixed shoots, some as tall as a man,
and miles of them going back into another century
of uniform labor the color of earth.
Anyone can break the code to take out the truth
because it is there, so long as there is an eye.
Language is different. History chokes on a rag of kerosene
the fuse is lit down a corridor of echoing images
and one cannot shuffe the fulgurating words
to nominate as aesthetics what time calls blood—
though once, it was thought, once—and a woman
doubled over and coughing must signal the scar
of cutlasses, diseases of the womb that maim the adult.
What do the fields represent, the harvest?
ratios, roads, drainage—the plucked flower of science—
these words are fuel to tinder, they promise
extremes of hatred if not boredom with the text
we were born to imitate, and that's the paradox
of being from an offshore rock: how to put out
the wide savagery when you're inside the beast
that in other legends, as wolf, swallows the community
in this one has left prints in the form of sugar cane
that actually broaches a goddess of slave economy.

Arachis Hypogaea → *scientific name*

> Great Creator, why
> did you make the peanut?
> — GWC

Arachis hypogaea may have been
smuggled to North America by slaves
who hid seeds of survival in their hair.
Despite your nakedness, the chains, the stench,
if white men did not eat you, you might come
to a cruel land where, tended by moonlight
and exhaustion, your seed might grow to be
your children's manna in the wilderness.

Arachis hypogaea, or goober,
an annual preferring warmth and sun,
is an attractive plant, resembling clover.
It bears flowers of two distinct genders:
the staminate, or "male," yellow, pretty,
and the inconspicuous pistillate "female."
When fertilized, the pistillate turns down
and corkscrews six inches into the ground.

Each corkscrew, called a "peg," grows one to four
peanuts in the soil near the mother plant;
each shell two of her shots at infinity.
From the laboratory of a slave emerged
a varied, balanced diet for the poor,
stock foods, ink, paints, cosmetics, medicines . . .
Promise and purpose, the Ancestors' dream.
"The Peanut Man," we say, and laugh at him.

In the Rachel Carson Wildlife Refuge, Thinking of Rachel Carson

The elements raveling and unraveling:
groundwater misting into rain, falling

back into groundwater; salt water wash
through brackish freshwater bordering

sea; we two wandering in late March
along the upland, among evergreens

and bare deciduous and bushes held fast
by the last of the snow, the rush and bubble

of the tidal river winding through low tide,
salt hay, cord and spike grass, walking

the path between firm ground and marsh.
The first time down the path leads

to enlightenment, the second, to wonder;
the third finds us silent, listening

to the few gulls lift and caw as we watch
the wind, which makes itself known

in the sea grass and as it dimples the water,
skimming like sunlight until a Coast Guard

chopper drowns for a moment the drone
of cars and trucks in the distance.

Language

Silence is one part of speech, the war cry
of wind down a mountain pass another.
A stranger's voice echoing through lonely
valleys, a lover's voice rising so close
it's your own tongue: these are keys to cipher,
the way the high hawk's key unlocks the throat
of the sky and the coyote's yip knocks
it shut, the way the aspens' bells conform
to the breeze while the rapid's drum defines
resistance. Sage speaks with one voice, pinyon
with another. Rock, wind her hand, water
her brush, spells and then scatters her demands.
Some notes tear and pebble our paths. Some notes
gather: the bank we map our lives around.

JUNE JORDAN

For Alice Walker
(a summertime tanka)

Redwood grove and war
You and me talking Congo
gender grief and ash

I say, "God! It's all so huge"
You say, "These sweet trees: This tree"

generations

people who are going to be
in a few years
bottoms of trees
bear a responsibility to something
besides people

> *Nature will last,*
> *We will not.*
> *• IDEA that*
> *life continues*
> *beyond us*

        if it was only
you and me
sharing the consequences
it would be different
it would be just
generations of men

        but

this business of war
these war kinds of things
are erasing those natural
obedient generations
who ignored pride

        stood on no hind legs
        begged no water
        stole no bread
did their own things

and the generations of rice
of coal
of grasshoppers

by their invisibility
denounce us

Work

I won't look at her.
My body's been one
Solid motion from sunrise,
Leaning into the lawnmower's
Roar through pine needles
& crabgrass. Tiger-colored
Bumblebees nudge pale blossoms
Till they sway like silent bells
Calling. But I won't look.
Her husband's outside Oxford,
Mississippi, bidding on miles
Of timber. I wonder if he's buying
Faulkner's ghost, if he might run
Into Colonel Sartoris
Along some dusty road.
Their teenage daughter & son sped off
An hour ago in a red Corvette
For the tennis courts,
& the cook, Roberta,
Only works a half day
Saturdays. The antebellum house
Looms behind oak & pine
Like a secret, as quail
Flash through branches.
I won't look at her. Nude
On a hammock among elephant ears
& ferns, a pitcher of lemonade
Sweating like our skin.
Afternoon burns on the pool
Till everything's blue,

Till I hear Johnny Mathis
Beside her like a whisper.
I work all the quick hooks
Of light, the same unbroken
Rhythm my father taught me
Years ago: *Always give*
A man a good day's labor.
I won't look. The engine
Pulls me like a dare.
Scent of honeysuckle
Sings black sap through mystery,
Taboo, law, creed, what kills
A fire that is its own heart
Burning open the mouth.
But I won't look
At the insinuation of buds
Tipped with cinnabar.
I'm here, as if I never left,
Stopped in this garden,
Drawn to some Lotus-eater. Pollen
Explodes, but I only smell
Gasoline & oil on my hands,
& can't say why there's this bed
Of crushed narcissus
As if gods wrestled here.

ROSS GAY

Poem to My Child, If Ever You Shall Be

after Steve Scafidi

The way the universe sat waiting to become,
quietly, in the nether of space and time,

you too remain some cellular snuggle
dangling between my legs, curled in the warm

swim of my mostly quietest self. If you come to be—
and who knows?—I wonder, little bubble

of unbudded capillaries, little one ever aswirl
in my vascular galaxies, what would you think

of this world which turns itself steadily
into an oblivion that hurts, and hurts bad?

Would you curse me my careless caressing you
into this world or would you rise up

and mustering all your strength into that tiny throat
which one day, no doubt, would grow big and strong,

scream and scream and scream until you break the back of one injustice,
or at least get to your knees to kiss back to life

some road kill? I have so many questions for you,
for you are closer to me than anyone

has ever been, tumbling, as you are, this second,
through my heart's every chamber, your teeny mouth

singing along with the half-broke workhorse's steady boom and gasp.
And since we're talking today I should tell you,

though I know you sneak a peek sometimes
through your father's eyes, it's a glorious day,

and there are millions of leaves collecting against the curbs,
and they're the most delicate shade of gold

we've ever seen and must favor the transparent
wings of the angels you're swimming with, little angel.

And as to your mother—well, I don't know—
but my guess is that lilac bursts from her throat

and she is both honeybee and wasp and some kind of moan to boot
and probably she dances in the morning—

but who knows? You'll swim beneath that bridge if it comes.
For now let me tell you about the bush called honeysuckle

that the sad call a weed, and how you could push your little
sun-licked face into the throngs and breathe and breathe.

Sweetness would be your name, and you would wonder why
four of your teeth are so sharp, and the tiny mountain range

of your knuckles so hard. And you would throw back your head
and open your mouth at the cows lowing their human songs

in the field, and the pigs swimming in shit and clover,
and everything on this earth, little dreamer, little dreamer

of the new world, holy, every rain drop and sand grain and blade
of grass worthy of gasp and joy and love, tiny shaman,

tiny blood thrust, tiny trillion cells trilling and trilling,
little dreamer, little hard hat, little heartbeat,

little best of me.

To a Certain Lady, in Her Garden

for Anne Spencer

Lady, my lady, come from out the garden,
Clay-fingered, dirty-smocked, and in my time
I too shall learn the quietness of Arden,
Knowledge so long a stranger to my rhyme.

What were more fitting than your springtime task?
Here, close-engirdled by your vines and flowers
Surely there is no other grace to ask,
No better cloister from the bickering hours.

A step beyond, the dingy streets begin
With all their farce, and silly tragedy—
But here, unmindful of the futile din
You grow your flowers, far wiser certainly.

You and your garden sum the same to me,
A sense of strange and momentary pleasure,
And beauty snatched—oh, fragmentarily
Perhaps, yet who can boast of other seizure?

Oh, you have somehow robbed, I know not how,
The secret of the loveliness of these
Whom you have served so long. Oh, shameless, now
You flaunt the winnings of your thieveries.

Thus, I exclaim against you, profiteer . . . .
For purpled evenings spent in pleasing toil,
Should you have gained so easily the dear
Capricious largesse of the miser soil?

Colorful living in a world grown dull,
Quiet sufficiency in weakling days,
Delicate happiness, more beautiful
for lighting up belittered, grimy ways—

Surely I think I shall remember this,
You in your old, rough dress, bedaubed with clay,
Your smudgy face parading happiness,
Life's puzzle solved. Perhaps, in turn, you may

One time, while clipping bushes, tending vines,
(Making your brave, sly mock at dastard days),
Laugh gently at these trivial, truthful lines—
And that will be sufficient for my praise.

ED ROBERSON

Urban Nature

Neither New Hampshire nor Midwestern farm,
nor the summer home in some Hamptons garden
thing, not that Nature, not a satori
-al leisure come to terms peel by peel, not that core
whiff of beauty as the spirit. Just a street
pocket park, clean of any smells, simple quiet—
simple quiet not the same as no birds sing,
definitely not the dead of no birds sing:

The bus stop posture in the interval
of nothing coming, a not quite here running
sound underground, sidewalk's grate vibrationless
in open voice, sweet berries ripen in the street
hawk's kiosks. The orange is being flown in
this very moment picked of its origin.

REGINALD SHEPHERD

September Songs

1
As we drove home through sun
-drowned afternoon, two immature white
ibises (brown with a touch
of gray, white throats, white heads, or so
you said, though I saw only dun and dark)
foraged a flooded field beside the turn-off
to the Mississippi Welcome Center, next rest
area 65 miles. Recent rain had made a lake
of lawn between three trees (the rain itself
gone for days), some temporary
roadside eden. I asked you
what they were and you pointed out
two snowy egrets, my birds
mere background, shadows
of that white poise, picking their way
through shallow and shallower
days. You didn't see the ibises
until we left, couldn't name my
descriptions, describing names
I knew already. It's a long, long way.

2
We have seen occasion and moved on,
the curtain of rain descends again
(some sound of water falling):

torn screen door, torn paper hat,
a torn black plastic garbage bag
ballooned in a corner of the front yard

while trees engage in their seasonal murder
of leaves, the ovate brittle ocher evidence
littering lawns and driveways. Backyard

mower mulch and ornamental elephant
ears, a white tool shed painted
off-white, grass after grass until there's nothing

to be seen. I pull rain through dry fingers,
dry hair and dry eyes; leaves'
tapered drip points bow to wet weather.

3

The nothing that's always happening,
sirens and the jaded sea, a fire somewhere
I can't see (some smoke
gets in my ears), an ambulance
demanding right of way on Nine Mile
Road to someone's near-fatal
accident, dressed up in mortality
and tinted coins of safety glass,
a creased and crumpled car
with a Jesus fish hooked to the trunk
gasping for air. I pull over to the side
and watch emergency pass on
its soundtrack for the present tense,
continue on my way to walking
the beach where green waves make time
out of tides and wind, color so true
it looks artificial, sand shuffing up
and down the slope into the Gulf,
engulfed and then released, uncertain
whether to drink or to drown.

CYCLE THREE

Dirt on Our Hands

RICHARD WRIGHT

from 12 *Million Black Voices*

The land we till is beautiful, with red and black and brown clay, with fresh and hungry smells, with pine trees and palm trees, with rolling hills and swampy delta—an unbelievably fertile land, bounded on the north by the states of Pennsylvania, Ohio, Illinois, and Indiana, on the south by the Gulf of Mexico, on the west by the Mississippi River, and on the east by the Atlantic Ocean.

Our southern springs are filled with quiet noises and scenes of growth. Apple buds laugh into blossom. Honeysuckles creep up the sides of houses. Sunflowers nod in the hot fields. From mossy tree to mossy tree—oak, elm, willow, aspen, sycamore, dogwood, cedar, walnut, ash, and hickory— bright green leaves jut from a million branches to form an awning that tries to shield and shade the earth. Blue and pink kites of small boys sail in the windy air.

In summer the magnolia trees fill the countryside with sweet scent for long miles. Days are slumberous, and the skies are high and thronged with clouds that ride fast. At midday the sun blazes and bleaches the soil. Butterflies flit through the heat; wasps sing their sharp, straight lines; birds fluff and flounce, piping in querulous joy. Nights are covered with canopies sometimes blue and sometimes black, canopies that sag low with ripe and nervous stars. The throaty boast of frogs momentarily drowns out the call and counter-call of crickets.

In autumn the land is afire with color. Red and brown leaves lift and flutter dryly, becoming entangled in the stiff grass and cornstalks. Cotton is picked and ginned; cane is crushed and its juice is simmered down into molasses; yams are grubbed out of the clay; hogs are slaughtered and cured in lingering smoke; corn is husked and ground into meal. At twilight the sky is full of wild geese winging ever southward, and bats jerk through the air. At night the winds blow free.

In winter the forests resound with the bite of steel axes eating into tall trees as men gather wood for the leaden days of cold. The guns of hunters snap and crack. Long days of rain come, and our swollen creeks rush to join a hundred rivers that wash across the land and make great harbors where they feed the gulf or the sea. Occasionally the rivers leap their banks and leave new thick layers of silt to enrich the earth, and then the look of the land is garish, bleak, suffused with a first-day stillness, strangeness, and awe.

But whether in spring or summer or autumn or winter, time slips past us remorselessly, and it is hard to tell of the iron that lies beneath the surface of our quiet, dull days.

To paint the picture of how we live on the tobacco, cane, rice, cotton plantations is to compete with mighty artists: the movies, the radio, the newspapers, the magazines, and even the Church. They have painted one picture: idyllic, romantic; but we live another; full of fear of the Lords of the Land, bowing and grinning when we meet white faces, toiling from sun to sun, living in unpainted wooden shacks that sit casually and insecurely upon the red clay.

In the main we are different from other folk in that, when an impulse moves us, when we are caught in the throes of inspiration, when we are moved to better our lot, we do not ask ourselves: "Can we do it?" but: "Will they let us do it?" Before we black folk can move, we must first look into the white man's mind to see what is there, to see what he is thinking, and the white man's mind is a mind that is always changing.

In general there are three classes of men above us: the Lords of the Land—operators of the plantations; the Bosses of the Buildings—the owners of industry; and the vast numbers of poor white workers—our immediate competitors in the daily struggle for bread. The Lords of the Land hold sway over the plantations and over us; the Bosses of the Buildings lend money and issue orders to the Lords of the Land. The Bosses of the Buildings feed upon the Lords of the Land, and the Lords of the Land feed upon the 5,000,000 landless poor whites and upon us, throwing to the poor whites the scant solace of filching from us 4,000,000 landless blacks what the poor whites themselves are cheated of in this elaborate game.

Back of this tangled process is a long history. When the Emancipation Proclamation was signed, there were some 4,000,000 of us black folk stranded and bewildered upon the land which we had tilled under compulsion for two and a half centuries. Sundered suddenly from the only relationship with Western civilization we had been allowed to form since our captivity, our personalities blighted by two hundred and fifty years of servitude, and eager to hold our wives and husbands and children together in family units, some if us turned back to the same Lords of the Land who had held us as slaves and begged for work, resorted to their advice; and there began for us a new kind of bondage: share cropping.

ANNE SPENCER

Another April

She is too weak to tend
her garden last year, this
year—and old.
The plants know, and
cluster, running free.
The wisteria, purple and white,
leaps from tree to martin-
box dragged down by globes
of the fragrant wet petals
to shore up, strengthen the vine, then
drops to touch Earth, to shoot
up again looping, hanging,
pealing out "April again!"
April is here! . . .
And the window from
which she stares needs washing—

Barriers

I go out for the news this morning
and find what's left of the slaughtered bird,
guts and wings, on my walk.
I know what did this.
There is someone's black and white cat
that hunts the woods back of our house,
stalking beyond the fence and stealing
some of my admiration for its great cousins
who bring down prey twice their size;
or it perches on a stump
that's a throne among the weeds, a power
in its dominion, but so visible
that I'd wondered if it ever made a kill.
Now here's the proof at my feet
in these black and white wings.
Today I take my stand against relativists
who reduce moral questions to shades of gray.
Things like this belong in the woods,
and that creature has no right to bring its savagery
across the fence and leave it at my door.
I sweep the thing into the grass
before pregnant Helen sees it.
The ants have already started arriving.
It all bothers my stomach at first, but it helps
to see it as a little chicken.
Like the kind we sometimes dress for dinner.

A Young Peacock

A young peacock preens
behind the splintered barn.

My old bulldog spies him.
The frightened peacock's feathers tremble
as he flees.
I smack Spike sharply on his nose.
I am angry, even ashamed.

Afternoon passes,
dusk slowly comes, keeping quiet.
The young peacock returns
mingles with the white chickens
while I gather their new eggs.

Urban Renewal

XIII

The backyard garden wall is mossy green
and flakes a craggy mound of chips. Nearby
my grandfather kneels between a row of beans
and stabs his shears into earth. I squint an eye,—
a comma grows at his feet. The stucco's
an atlas, meshed-wire continents with leaders
who augured hate, hence ruins, which further sow
discontent. We are weeding, marking borders,
a million taproots stacked in shock. Forty years
from a three-story, he has watched the neighborhood,—
postwar marble steps, a scrubbed frontier
of Pontiacs lining the curb, fade to a hood.
Pasture of wind-driven litter swirls among greasy
bags of takeouts. Panicles of nightblasts
cap the air, a corner lot of broken TVs empties
and spills from a suitcase of hurt. Life amassed,
meaningless as a trampled box of Cornflakes.
When a beggar cupped for change outside
a check-cashing place then snatched his wallet,
he cleaned a .22 revolver & launched this plot. Tidal
layers of cement harden men born gentle as the root
crops tended south, the city its own bitter shrine.
We crouch by watering cans. He pulls a paradise of kale
and shakes root-dirt that snaps like a shadow lost in time.
Tomato vines coil by a plot of herbs. Far from the maddening
caravan of fistfights, jacked-rides, drunkards,
my pen takes aim from the thumbnail of his yard.

The Bees

In the street outside a school
what the children learn
possesses them.
Little boys yell as they stone a flock of bees
trying to swarm
between the lunchroom window and an iron grate.
The boys sling furious rocks
smashing the windows.
The bees, buzzing their anger,
are slow to attack.
Then one boy is stung
into quicker destruction
and the school guards come
long wooden sticks held out before them
they advance upon the hive
beating the almost finished rooms of wax apart
mashing the new tunnels in
while fresh honey drips
down their broomsticks
and the little boy feet becoming expert
in destruction
trample the remaining and bewildered bees
into the earth.

Curious and apart
four little girls look on in fascination
learning a secret lesson
and trying to understand their own destruction.
One girl cries out

[handwritten annotations: "word choice", "author sympathizes w/ bees", "beat hives not perpetrators", "word choice"]

"Hey, the bees weren't making any trouble!"
and she steps across the feebly buzzing ruins
to peer up at the empty, grated nook
"We could have studied honey-making!"

Carrion

Headless deer
               at milepost 55

something like a beaver at the bridge
over Route 83

smashed meat and bone beyond recognition
on the ramp to the frontage road

to the mall, beyond

there the plowed under, paved
over fields—

           Beaver Ridge,
Houston Farms, Woodland Acres—

denuded and flat farmlands dreamt
into grids of Fox
             Hills and Apple
Valley, linked and speared by channeled
clearcuts linking cities, linking

natural to development

states, roads—88, 101, 95 accumulate
and stack like suburbs
on the horizons, while

raccoons lie blankly beside
porcupines; labyrinthine mess

of intestines, hair, eyes there
or not there, glowing

reflected light every half mile

Deer Park, Beaver Ridge, Forest Glen, Indian
Ridge

look at the blackbird fall

look at the blackbird fall
down
into the lake
split white speedboats full of white people
loading the atmosphere with gasoline
and noise
now
you can't drink the water
of the lake
you must drive somewhere else to buy
bottles of water to drink
beside the lake that is ten miles
long
(what I need is a change of season
a snowmobile
or a springtime tomb
that takes me from birth to 55
in six seconds)

fantasy

reality

what I need is to adjust
to the tree
without the blackbird that fell
down
into the lake

Flight of the California Condor

for you, los angeles—you at my jugular

wind sistuh blooded eyes
mind full of flesh

> womb/dark moist
> unknown walls suck you
> so deep down
> you become lost
> die there

what the eyes tell him he senses, the way the rabbit pursuit
descent out of sky, claws/talons—*snatch*. he's
helpless, midair, familiar ground gives way this alien sky
ahead, the nest and death. he is fed to the young

breaker breaker
this is the hollywatts kid comin' at yah

steadily they grow. strong, vibrant, vital. they curl and
uncurl, test their environs. cry of discovery. something
inside hungers to wing free

> at the party the wealthy white bridge
> champion followed me from one chair to the
> next. "tell me what did I do? *what did I do?*
> the three black ones i loved hurt me
> what did i do? they took my money
> and left. why?"

here on this plain, constant thunder. no rain. the sky
seems pregnant, about to burst, enraged. but no. only the
splash-lash of lightning opening up corners of the room
dispelling shadows for a second. long into day it can be heard
for miles—thunder/the heart embedded in the groin of fear

> at the office he came to tell me how much
> we had in common. classical music,
> writing, intelligence. "if
> you'll forgive me, we must be soul mates,"
> and in his eyes and in his wife's eyes the
> mattress waited, convulsed with our flesh
> entwined. taste of me on his tongue, and hers
> what would it be like entering me, fucking
> my soul. i said no. he tried to get me fired

wing spread like a condor. the multicolored feather coat. rare
bird this. it burns/an unanswered question, is as inaccessible
as the planet's heart, preens and struts, avoids capture. like the
horizon—is never reached

break into me, break into me
this earth has never been violated

> it expands to welcome, closes
> clangs/bolts/lockup
> in county jail
> imprisoned, he moves
> to tear free

like quicksand, she appears harmless, ordinary, calm. he
didn't recognize until he was up to his nose in her, seeing
too late. either to be pulled suddenly, violently free or
expire in that hole

> it labors. contracts. gives out.
> screams dance in her lungs

                    pepper the page
                    so many ink blots/a drop
                    on him shrivels him up like
                    a slug under salt

"if i had known i was going to die in california, i'd never have
come here," his few belongings hastily packed. the guitar across
his back. taking a vacation, not knowing there would be nothing to
come back to except his old army picture dangling from the bedroom
wall. she would be gone and all traces of their life together

there's nothing delicate here. delicate
things do not survive. they get beaten up/raped/shot/
runover/knifed/poisoned or pushed into suicide
they harden, become brittle, or bend
baked under sun of years, adobe will not
yield to crop, but brick to build—
where the farmer fails, the architect prospers: a city

(one day we will plow you under and dance the ritual of your passing)

under quicksand she waits. how long before he discovers
it's a movie prop/emerges a bit confused, perhaps embarrassed but
alive to find the treasure of her embrace, test passed
successfully. but he drops to her feet a corpse/choked on fear
angrily she rewrites the script for the next actor

                    i am dressed in a thin lavender negligee
                    crouched behind the door. he moves past me onto
                    the porch to see if i've escaped. spits a curse
                    and stomps drunk, upstairs. i flee. the children/he
                    won't hurt the children, can't hurt the children
                    but he'll kill me so i run, feet bare against
                    sidewalk/glass rock bottle cap bite my feet
                    draw blood. i run to brother love's
                    beat on his door until he stirs. he allows me
                    sanctuary and the employ of his tub

break me open, break me open
white on the outside, rich warm chocolate inside

these streets are lean, familiar faces in bitter forms that
dot doorways, cluster at corners, weave along the walk. i know
the pimp, the pootbutt, the whore, the worker, the blind, the
cowboy, the ditty-bop, the gangster, the hype, the hustler, the
young whites who visit the old whites who couldn't make the flight
exiled, the ghetto becomes home

> the adjective bank is empty
> the seer's tongue ensconced in
> a coat of cryptic truths
> her fingers/talons wet with
> blood of capture
> having plucked him from
> the desert's floor

mother of angels let me burn forever in the oven of your love

Since Everyone Can Never Be Safe

The bitch ran in the pack
      and nothing about that was remarkable
      except the sight of her intestines on the ground as well as in her gut.

But we were yakking about kids before we turned to dogs.
      They were playing, what d'you call that game?
Kids scattered in pairs across the yard, elbows linked, the lot of them,

      except the one who was it and one other one.
We were working fifty weeks a year now, adult hours.
These dinners were a decadence we could easily afford.

      The loose toms and spayed pups we called our own,
      even they knew there was more than enough
            and no longer beat us to the bowls we filled two times each day.

If the kid who's it's too close the other kid'll grab some arm.
      Then the kid whose partner got the grab,
now he's got to be the one to run.

My friend, she'd seen those dogs and had, that night,
      though I'm sure we hadn't asked her,
      to tell us about them.

The thing that got me was these kids,
they kept screaming,
      Trevor, Trevor, Trevor,

and holding out their arms.
Then it was Maria,
  Maria, Maria, *when Trevor grabbed someone.*

Most of us had been to the place she was talking about.
  God it was hot,
one of us remembered.

  Oh, and that flat bread!
We said, remember the west bank
  of the river? How lazy that afternoon was?

They'd yell, Maria, Maria,
and wave their little arms,
  though any arm that got the grab, that meant some other kid would have
    to run.

Dinner that night, if I can recall, consisted of several courses:
    Lamb shank on a bed of cracked barley, chickpeas, home-cured
      olives, a chutney or two;

    arugula salad with cashews and organic tomatoes;
  thick-crusted bread; a healthy soup;
  something sweet to top it off; a plenitude of wine.

It was only the way she dragged herself along the street my friend
  remembered.
Like she was all together and not dripping apart.
  Not dragging her own stomach down the road.

It was only the way that bitch acted.
How normal she made all of it seem.
  Nothing remarkable. Those dogs. Their hunger.

I mean, what were they, really, what were they looking to do?
Even the way they consumed the bitch,
  those dogs.

My friend wanted us to see how easy it seemed,
watching all of this go down. That pack was unremarkable.
   She almost overlooked them, really.

   The way they got behind her and on top.
   That every one was eating.
Nothing could be less remarkable than that.

Won't Be But a Minute

August 25, 2007

Tie Luther B to that cypress. He gon' be alright.
That dog done been rained on before,
he done been here a day or two by hisself before,
and we sho' can't take him. Just leave him
some of that Alpo and plenty of water.
Bowls and bowls of water.
We gon' be back home soon this thing pass over.
Luther B gon' watch the place while we gone.
You heard the man—he said *Go*—and you know
white folks don't warn us 'bout nothing unless
they scared too. We gon' just wait this storm out.
Then we come on back home. Get our dog.

MICHAEL S. HARPER

Called

in memoriam, L. G. Buffington, 1942–2008

Digging the grave
through black dirt,
gravel and rocks
that will hold her down,
we speak of her heat
which has driven her out
over the highway
in her first year.

A fly glides from her mouth
as we take her four legs,
and the great white neck
muddled at the lakeside
bends gracefully into the arc
of her tongue, colorless, now,
and we set her in the bed
of earth and rock
which will hold her as the sun
sets over her shoulders.

You had spoken of her brother,
100 lbs or more,
and her slight frame
from the diet of chain
she had broken;
on her back
as the spade cools her brow
with black dirt, rocks,

sand, white tongue,
what pups does she hold
that are seeds unsprayed
in her broken body;
what does her brother say
to the seed gone out over
the prairie, on the hunt
of the unreturned:
and what do we say
to the master of the dog dead,
heat, highway, this bed
on the shoulder
of the road west
where her brother called, calls.

JEAN TOOMER

Harvest Song

I am a reaper whose muscles set at sundown. All my oats are cradled.
But I am too chilled, and too fatigued to bind them. And I hunger.

I crack a grain between my teeth. I do not taste it.
I have been in the fields all day. My throat is dry. I hunger.

My eyes are caked with dust of oatfields at harvest-time.
I am a blind man who stares across the hills, seeking stack'd fields of other
    harvesters.

It would be good to see them . . crook'd, split, and iron-ring'd handles of the
    scythes. It would be good to see them, dust-caked and blind. I hunger.

(Dusk is a strange fear'd sheath their blades are dull'd in.)
My throat is dry. And should I call, a cracked grain like the oats . . . eoho—

I fear to call. What should they hear me, and offer me their grain, oats, or
    wheat, or corn? I have been in the fields all day. I fear I could not taste it.
    I fear knowledge of my hunger.

My ears are caked with dust of oatfields at harvest-time.
I am a deaf man who strains to hear the calls of other harvesters whose
    throats are also dry.

It would be good to hear their songs . . reapers of the sweet-stalk'd
    cane, cutters of the corn . . even though their throats cracked and the
    strangeness of their voices deafened me.

I hunger. My throat is dry. Now that the sun has set and I am chilled, I fear
    to call. (Eoho, my brothers!)

I am a reaper. (Eoho!) All my oats are cradled. But I am too fatigued to bind them. And I hunger. I crack a grain. It has no taste to it. My throat is dry . . .

O my brothers, I beat my palms, still soft, against the stubble of my harvesting. (You beat your soft palms, too.) My pain is sweet. Sweeter than the oats or wheat or corn. It will not bring me knowledge of my hunger.

A Black Man Talks of Reaping

I have sown beside all waters in my day.
I planted deep, within my heart the fear
that wind or fowl would take the grain away.
I planted safe against this stark, lean year.

I scattered seed enough to plant the land
in rows from Canada to Mexico
but for my reaping only what the hand
can hold at once is all that I can show.

Yet what I sowed and what the orchard yields
my brother's sons are gathering stalk and root;
small wonder then my children glean in fields
they have not sown, and feed on bitter fruit.

MELVIN DIXON

Wood and Rain

I am black man of woods
weeping
where old trees root
like men
hollering
in the wind
for lost children,
where folds of knotted skin
break off
and stab the ground, and fat
black fingers
sky-scratch a warning:

*there is no hiding, there is no home
in wet woods or this soil.*

Here a leaf
drops like a dead bird.
Listen, the woods weep.
My fingers grip the dirt where I fall.

Joy in the Woods

There is joy in the woods just now,
    The leaves are whispers of song,
And the birds <u>make mirth on the bough</u>
    And music the whole day long,
And God! to dwell in the town
    In these springlike summer days,
On my brow an unfading frown
    And hate in my heart always—

A machine out of gear, aye, tired,   *compare self*
Yet forced to go on—for I'm hired.   *to machine*

Just forced to go on through fear,
    For every day I must eat
And find ugly clothes to wear,
    And bad shoes to hurt my feet
And a shelter for work-drugged sleep!
    A mere drudge! but what can one do?
A man that's a man cannot weep!
    Suicide? A quitter? Oh, no!

But a slave should never grow tired,
Whom the masters have kindly hired.

But oh! for the woods, the flowers
    Of natural, sweet perfume,
The heartening, summer showers
    And the smiling shrubs in bloom,
Dust free, dew tinted at morn,
    The fresh and life-giving air,

The billowing waves of corn
  And the birds' notes rich and clear:—

For a man-machine toil-tired
May crave beauty too—though he's hired.

↳ idea of fear & fatigue, but
still appreciates surrounding
nature, non-human life
forms

Sorrow Home

My roots are deep in southern life; deeper than John Brown
        or Nat Turner or Robert Lee. I was sired and weaned
        in a tropic world. The palm tree and banana leaf,
        mango and coconut, breadfruit and rubber trees know me.

Warm skies and gulf blue streams are in my blood. I belong
        with the smell of fresh pine, with the trail of coon, and
        the spring growth of wild onion.

I am no hothouse bulb to be reared in steam-heated flats
        with the music of El and subway in my ears, walled in
        by steel and wood and brick far from the sky.

I want the cotton fields, tobacco and the cane. I want to
        walk along with sacks of seed to drop in fallow ground.
        Restless music is in my heart and I am eager to be gone.

O Southland, sorrow home, melody beating in my bone and
        blood! How long will the Klan of hate, the hounds and
        the chain gangs keep me from my own?

love of land, history & culture
↳ especially in background/
individual sense

clouded by owners, settlers (etc)

HONORÉE FANONNE JEFFERS

Blues Aubade (or, Revision of the Lean, Post-Modernist Pastorale)

I'm going to work in the holy name of Cézanne
somewhere in here, but first, let's say

I take a walk with my spade to safe, blank territory,
and then surely I'll dig to distraction in spongy loam,

then see petals spread, a chorus round a lazy eye,
then reach an epiphany—the importance of memory—

which necessitates a recollection of a lover
lying on a bed sheet,

his sparrow-boned hand gesturing vaguely toward me.
At this point there is early light filtering through a glass

of wine so clean, almost white on the bedside table.
Then I'll find a reason to conjure Cézanne—

Cézanne! Cézanne! Cézanne!—
as my excuse to discuss the poems he painted on canvas.

Before I start meditating on the apple's green buttock,
I hope there is time for a second walk

to another field that breaks me down, for prayer
and work, the precarious undoing of my birth.

Boss man calling me out of my name, hoe
over my shoulder to attack the hard crust.

Some cotton, some peaches, weighty heat of this harvest—
I remember my baby when we parted this morning.

We loved, we cried, O never enough!
We squeezed the scuppernong into spirit, drank it down gladly.

Brother Bearden had a relief for this kind of life,
a collage of agrarian truths. In this picture,

see the woman carved into the foreground of sweat?
And there—over *there*—way in the corner?

Now, that's a rooster crowing up a revolution.

ED ROBERSON

romance

it is known why the farmers
desert that fondling of their fields
why their wives give up the chickens
to the sly night that ferrets
the moon egg in the trough from between
the legs of the fence it is now
known why the children are hushed in
behind the lamps and the horses
excuse themselves into inconspicuous tufts
in the field's sleep because
it is embarrassing
this romance of empty space
that makes the open smell
of cowshit so untouchably near
that the white silo in the next farm
sweats with moonlight and accidentally
spills a slight stream of corn

ALICE DUNBAR-NELSON

April Is on the Way

April is on the way!
I saw the scarlet flash of a blackbird's wing
As he sang in the cold, brown February trees;
And children said that they caught a glimpse
Of the sky on a bird's wing from the far South.
(Dear God, was that a stark figure outstretched in the bare branches
Etched brown against the amethyst sky?)

April is on the way!
The ice crashed in the brown mud-pool under my tread,
The warning earth clutched my bloody feet with great fecund fingers.
I saw a boy rolling a hoop up the road,
His little bare hands were red with cold,
But his brown hair blew backward in the southwest wind.
(Dear God! He screamed when he saw my awful woe-spent eyes.)

April is on the way!
I met a woman in the lane;
Her burden was heavy as it is always, but today her step was light,
And a smile drenched the tired look away from her eyes.
(Dear God, she had dreams of vengeance for her slain mate,
Perhaps the west wind has blown the mist of hate from her heart,
The dead man was cruel to her, you know that, God.)

April is on the way!
My feet spurn the ground now, instead of dragging on the bitter road.

"April Is on the Way" is from *Works of Alice Dunbar-Nelson*, vol. 2, ed.
G. T. Hull, © 1988 by Oxford University Press. Reprinted by permission of
Oxford University Press, Inc.

I laugh in my throat as I see the grass greening beside the patches of snow
(Dear God, those were wild fears. Can there be hate
When the southwest wind is blowing?)

April is on the way!
The crisp brown hedges stir with the bustle of bird wings.
There is business of building, and songs from brown thrush throats
As the bird-carpenters make homes against Valentine's Day.
(Dear God, could they build me a shelter in the hedge
From the icy winds that will come with the dark?)

April is on the way!
I sped through the town this morning.
The florist shops have put yellow flowers in the windows,
Daffodils and tulips and primroses, pale and yellow flowers,
Like the tips of her fingers when she waved me that frightened farewell.
And the women in the market have stuck pussy willows
In long-necked bottles on their stands
(Willow trees are kind, Dear God. They will not bear a body on their limbs.)

April is on the way!
The soul within me cried that all the husk of indifference to sorrow
Was but the crust of ice with which winter disguises life;
It will melt, and reality will burgeon forth like the crocuses in the glen.
(Dear God! Those thoughts were from long ago, when we read poetry
After the day's toil, and got religion together at the revival meeting.)

April is on the way!
The infinite miracle of unfolding life in the brown February fields.
(Dear God, the hounds are baying!)
Murder and wasted love, lust and weariness, deceit and vainglory—
What are they but the spent breath of the runner?
(God, you know he laid hairy red hands on the golden loveliness of her little
    daffodil body.)
Hate may destroy me, but from my brown limbs will bloom
The golden buds with which we once spelled love.
(Dear God! How their light eyes glow into black pin points of hate!)

April is on the way!

Wars are made in April, and they sing at Easter time of the Resurrection.

Therefore I laugh in their faces.

(Dear God, give her strength to join me before her golden petals are fouled
   in the slime!)

April is on the way!

Pests, People Too

Boll Weevils, Coyotes, and the Color of Nuisance

Histories of "The Boll Weevil Song" tend to lead back to Charlie Patton (1891–1934) and his 1929 performance of "Mississippi Bo Weavil Blues" under the name Masked Marvel at Paramount's Gennett Studios in Richmond, Indiana. The sobriquet was a Paramount sales ploy—a free record would be awarded to anyone correctly guessing the Masked Marvel's identity. The song has been covered and modified by any number of folks since then—Leadbelly, Woody Guthrie, Bessie Smith, the White Stripes, among many others.

In the lyrics, a farmer and a boll weevil square off about a piece of land and the cotton on it: the farmer catalogs the ways in which he's tried to destroy the weevil, to make the environment uninhabitable for the insect and its offspring (the eggs are laid inside the plants), but the weevil replies that he'll make himself a home-place—that he'll make himself *at home*—no matter what the farmer does. It's a call-and-response song, a verbal sparring contest.

And there was truth there—the weevil's with us still. Weevils, at maturity, are a scant quarter-inch long but quite capable, in numbers, of laying waste to a cotton crop. A 2003 USDA bulletin, leaning on Carl Sandburg's version of the song for an epigraph, made this unironic observation: "Since its entry into the United States from Mexico in 1892, the insect scientifically known as *Anthonomus grandis* Boheman spread throughout the South, forcing radical economic and social changes in areas that had been almost completely dependent on cotton production. Many experts consider the boll weevil second only to the Civil War as an agent of change in the South." And the insect, like the Civil War, has had different levels of meaning for the black southerners who *worked* the fields than it's had for the white captains of industry who *owned* the fields. There are lots of ways to configure "home."

I heard the song at ten, in the spring of 1961. Hospitalized for months then, the result of an unlikely injury—a backyard fall—I lived by my radio and learned the words to all the music on the Top Forty, including Brook Benton's "Boll Weevil Song" (which made it to number two). I was drawn to the spoken interplay, the dialogue—with Benton's smooth, familiar voice taking both parts—and especially to the sung refrain's changes: "Gotta have a home" (in the weevil's strident voice at the beginning) becomes "Ah, you have a home all right, you have a home" (in the farmer's grudging tone) by the end of the record. Re-encountering the song in other versions, including Charlie Patton's, in the years after that, I liked more and more the complex metaphoric action I'd sensed at ten—man and weevil are both homeless but at odds, profoundly alike and profoundly different. Their places in the song shift, their voices come a little undone—I was ten when I heard it first, but I saw it was different than other songs on the radio, and I count "The Boll Weevil Song" as being among my early encounters with the stuff of poetry. In those later years, I also came to understand the song's wide appeal—worker populations, white and black, were shifted by weevil infestations, and signature lines in the lyrics varied interestingly (and were interestingly similar). From an Oklahoma Co-operative Extension publication:

> Now if anyone should ask you
> Who it was that wrote this here song,
> You can say it was just a homeless Farmer
> with ragged britches on,
> Just hunting for a home, yes, hunting for a home.

And this transcription from the "Great Migration" Web site at the University of Illinois:

> An', if anybody should ax you
> Who it was dat make dis song,
> Jus' tell 'em 'twas a big buck niggah
> Wid a paih o' blue duckin's on,
> Ain' got no home,
> Ain' got no home.

My sister and I were born in Ohio in the 1950s; we were northern city children. We lived in Dayton, on the West Side—all black Daytonians in the 1950s and '60s lived on the West Side, the neighborhoods on the west side of the Miami River. Our parents had come from the South, but we were distant from the old country and its traditions. We were a progressive family and this was the postwar prosperity; we were beyond familiarity with red dirt and cotton fields. We were Baby Boomers, we were trained to be polite; we listened to Top Forty radio and went downtown to the library and the big department stores, and we watched the Saturday matinees with the white children who lived across the Miami, a waterway we knew we could not cross casually; I mean we knew we had a different value—a different *meaning*—in the neighborhoods over there. But downtown was common ground, and in the downtown theaters I sat through *Bambi, Snow White*, and the loose-limbed jiving crows of *Dumbo;* watching TV at home, staying with the Disney industry, I caught the act of ineffectually wicked Br'er Fox and dim-witted Br'er Bear, seeing only much later their connection to both the minstrel tradition *and* the animal stories from black folklore. I came to the animal stories themselves after I was grown, in my thirties; I was teaching by then in universities and would cover a week or so of folklore as part of my course in African American literature. I argued in those classes for the primacy of the trickster figure, the figure often cast as a small animal (a rabbit, say, or a spider) or a marginal one (e.g., a coyote). We read beyond Joel Chandler Harris (whose Uncle Remus stories were an origin point for Disney's *Song of the South*), we read stories collected by Richard Dorson and published by Langston Hughes; I scandalized my students with "The Signifyin' Monkey." I sent them out to look at graffiti that someone had painted on a paved rail-trail near campus, part of the city's much-publicized Circle Greenway project: "Emerald Necklace? Feels more like an ass-fault choker to me, said Coyote."

Teaching the animal stories made me like and admire them—I fell hard for the stories, for the language I heard and saw there, the language that created them with repetitions and varieties of address. Reading them, I could hear the performance, I could feel the resonance with moments of speech in my own experience with black adults and children (including unguarded moments of my parents' speech). Everything connected—language, race, geography, animals in a variety of roles. And I recalled the farmer's complicated conversation with the boll weevil, the articulation of difference and confrontation that I'd first heard in a black voice at ten, in "a novelty song" on the radio.

Charlie Patton had sung and spoke thus:

> Bo weavil left Texas, Lord,
> he bid me "fare ye well," Lordie
> (spoken: Where you goin' now?)
> I'm goin' down the Mississippi, gonna give Louisiana hell, Lordie
> (spoken: How is that, boy?)
> Suck all the blossoms and he leave your hedges square, Lordie.

But we were far from all that as children and, later, as young profession-als in the 1980s and '90s, farther still—at least in our daily lives. We both left Dayton after high school but have visited frequently over the past forty years, have witnessed the inevitable economic and social changes. There's still an old-money neighborhood in Dayton where black people don't live—though, to be fair, my sister and I do shop there, when we're in town together, and eat at the fine restaurants on its main drag, Far Hills Avenue. Our Visa cards are welcomed and the waitresses are polite. I tend to "read" cities and locations as though they were poems—ambiguous, contradictory, riddled with echoes of other poems and other places. You can understand a place, in part, by the kind of animal life it supports (a sentiment not original with me). How might *all* a town's populations work their way into the big poem, the epic, of a par-ticular location? Or how might the populations resist the poem's definitions or prove more slippery than the demographic? And how can the sentimental be avoided?

November 2007 came and the Giscombe children were back in Dayton for a long weekend. Our parents were old and ill and we were in town to in-terview health care providers. One rainy evening, on the way back from an appointment, I pulled off onto the shoulder of a new highway so we could examine a piece of roadkill. This was Ohio Route 49 just below the intersec-tion with Little Richmond Road, the old way over to faded Indiana; this was the half-rural edge of the storied West Side, unchanged black Dayton, and my sister and I piled out to see that I'd been right—it was a coyote, *Canis latrans*, legs almost broken off, head half-smashed, the fur still beautiful in the rental car's headlights. They're western animals; I knew they'd been extending their range east for decades, but I'd not known they'd made it as far as Dayton, as far as the fields and scrubby woods and culverts between the houses and busi-nesses of the West Side. This was no trickster figure; Googling "coyote" and "Ohio" later, I found that there've been coyotes in Dayton for a while now and that in the state game laws they're a nuisance animal, an animal with "no closed season"—you can shoot a nuisance animal at any time. How'd this guy get here? Let music come up:

> First time I saw Mr. Boll Weevil,
> He wuz on de western plain;
> Next time I saw him,
> He wuz ridin' on a Memphis train.

I've taken pains to locate the coyote among us, but there's really no lesson in any of it, no complicated metaphor; and neither is this a poem about "swerving" or my heart being ambiguously "fastened to a dying animal." Location's a jumble of proximities and coincidence. Other coyotes were certainly alive, maybe to sing to me some evening, if discordantly, from black Dayton, from my old home.

Miscarriage in October with Ladybugs

Window dusk mobilizes each blood drop.
Miniscule as bunchberries, they gather on the blinds,
crowd a transparent diagram of ovaries, the uterus dappled

with the heart-shaped crawlers. The nurse's fingers
prod and flutter between tools on a silver tray.
"This will pinch." Karen, on last night's news

warned we were not going out of our minds—the pests
are harmless to wood, house plants, carpets.
The migration will be over in a week, before we know it.

My superstitious eye roves for meaning.
They are known as "God's beetles," "Our Lady's birds."
Soft cluck on the exam table's stiff paper. They land,

top-heavy spinners able to recover equilibrium
only when their wings, exploding like capped arms,
open out. The defining marks, the red of crab apples

split apart to reveal the furrowed body beneath.
I let one journey my arm. The tang of my apricot lotion
like sickness. Legs so delicate, it struggles

to cross my wristbone, barely pausing over a fleck
of a mole. I'm no station for this wayward seeker.
I shake my arm, blow the hairs to attention.

In the sterile spoon of a speculum, the bugs flicker in
and out of being. "This will sting." Yes, the walls are disaster,
always rearranging their evidence of loss. Not unlike

the iodine-soaked gauze the nurse drops in the waste can,
lid slapping shut. Hope takes so long to shut down. Then slow,
they retrace paths, stall on the stethoscope's flat ear,
search a way in a jar of cotton balls, that cornered heaven.

GREGORY PARDLO

Man Reading in Bed by a Window with Bugs

—a second floor window, darkened
but for a single lamp,
winged insects creep through a rift
in the screen as if seeking asylum
on the lamp's damp skiff of light.
the cicada's reporting ticker-tape
seems to augur a storm and a frayed cordage
of willow branch blanches in accord
and the brook nods, applauds. the book
is a cat in his lap as he nods
off and leaks through the frayed   → used of
screen down to where, in affection,   frayed
arches the tall grass the wind
strokes as oak leaves leather
in the yellow porch light and shine
dully. he sets off, each step toward the open
sounds like the turning of a page.
when the breeze wakes him he shuts the window,
still imagining himself shirtless in the field.
each pore is a teat, he thinks, each teat a socket
the night plugs in to power its miner's lamp   ♡
hung above oceans of talcum and calamine.

awareness of beasts & small
      demands
   poet of meditation
 └→ elemental point of view

Pest

I heard the terrible laughter of termites
deep inside a spray-painted wall on Sharswood.
My first thought was that of Swiss cheese
hardening on a counter at the American Diner.
My second thought was that of the senator
from Delaware on the senate floor.
I was on my way to the life of bagging tiny mountains,
selling poetry on the corners of North Philly,
a burden to mothers & Christians.
Hearing it, too, the cop behind me shoved me
aside for he was an entomologist
in a former lifetime & he knew the many
song structures of cicadas, bush crickets &
fruit flies. He knew the complex courtship
of bark beetles, how the male excavates
a nuptial chamber & buries himself—
his back end sticking out till a female sang
a lyric of such intensity he squirmed like a Quaker
& gave himself over to the quiet history
of trees & ontology. All this he said while
patting me down, slapping first my ribs, then
sliding his palms along the sad, dark shell
of my body.
       How lucky I was
spread-eagled at 13, discovering the ruinous cry
of insects as the night air flashed reds

& blues, as a lone voice chirped & cracked
over a radio; the city crumbling. We stood
a second longer sharing the deafening hum
of termites, back from their play & rest,
till he swung suddenly my right arm then my left.

Ambition II: Mosquito in the Mist

You human-types, you
two-legged sapien-sapiens,
you guys are walking smoothies
ta me, milkshakes wearin' trousers,
a cup'a coffee mowin' a lawn.

I gotta hand it to you though—
all the colors, the smells, tall,
petite, skinny-minnies or whoppin'
whale-sized motha'humphries—you
got variety: I'm zippin' around
some summa' nights and it's like
an all-you-can-eat situation.

And I like the threads—hiphop
baggies, halter tops, baseball caps,
culottes—stylin'! And
most'a the fabrics flexible enough
for me and my little straw.

But I sense some chronic
unfriendliness, some ongoing
agitation from you hemaglobes.
My family and me are small things
tryin'a quench a thirst. It's our nature.
The random violence is really
uncalled for. The bashing, the swatting . . .
And *the cursing*! Fuck you guys, man!
It's like you never heard'a the word
compromise.

And the worst
is when you bring down the curtain
right in the middle
of a good suck. I don't think
I need ta spotlight the obvious
analogy, but ok: imagine yourself
alone wit' someone you want

real bad—*her skin is toffee,*
his hair is an avalanche
of dreadlocks—and
the moment
comes: the shared
shimmer in the eyes and you
lean into the kiss, warm
and rich as God's
good cocoa, your mouth's
famished apparatus
slurping up the sweetness,

when—   a smack,
big as Godzilla, knocks the livin'
juji-fruit outta you.

The luscious touches, the hum
of two hearts, the holy
communion flung into the fat-ass dark forever.
What? You think we ain't
got feelings!? I got the memories.
It's all in the genes! See,
you big-holes-in-the-face motha'humphries
don't never think nothin'
about other kinds'a life,

but that's ah'ight, I got dreams. I got
big plans. I'm all itchy and bumpy
wit' discontent—and you might not

see it, but I'm gettin' bigger—I
been liftin'—and someday I'm gonna
get a little payback on the go:

land on your cheek like a
round-house kick, and before
you can pick up your nostrils
I'm gonna drink you dry, drain ya
to the lees—you'll be
layin' there stiff as beef jerky,
your arrogant balloon
all flat and wrinkly
while I lift off   like a, like a

helicopter, like a goddam
12-cylinda' angel, like a bulldozer
witta' probiskamus big
as a' elephant's dick.

RICHARD WRIGHT

#459

    I am paying rent
For the lice in my cold room
      And the moonlight too.

The Market

Our parents were thrilled when it reopened,
A place to buy fresh fruit, vegetables, and meat.
So nearby, our mothers practically rolled out of bed
Into the market then home into their kitchens or soaps.

Only God could save time, so we thanked Him—
Amen! But later for Him was casting a plague on us,
The rats and roaches that plotted while we were asleep—
How to get their claws and sharp teeth on our meat.

Both chicken and beef told on themselves when our mothers
Baked or boiled them. Like lust, the scent of flesh cooking
Attracted more of the same greedy occupants we already had.
Nightly, their eyes bulged and watered in the darkness

And in the cracks and crevices between our refrigerator
And stove, cabinets, and wall. They laid eggs
We couldn't eat where they thought we couldn't see
Or reach them. Their families outgrew ours.

Our holidays became theirs. The courageous ones
Would chance their lives scurrying across the floor
While we ate—blinded by the crumbs that fell
From our mouths into theirs like snow.

For Those Who Need a True Story

The landlord told Raymond's mother that twelve dollars
would be deducted from their rent for every rat killed.
She sends her son to the store for a loaf of Wonder Bread
and five pounds of ground beef. Young Raymond
returns with bread & meat that she tears & mixes inside
a metal bowl. Mama seasons this meatloaf with rat poison
pulled from the cabinet beneath the sink. Well done,
meat sits steaming in the middle of the kitchen floor.
Then the scratching scurries. The squeaking begins
and screeches toward the bowl.

Raymond describes the wave of rats like a tidal crash
covering the bowl, leaping over each other's bodies,
then the dropping, the stutter kicks.

A chorus of rat screams ramble through Raymond's ears.
Keening, furry bodies tense paws against churning guts
as they hit cracked linoleum until an hour passes.
Silence swept away the din in death's footsteps.
The mother's voice quivers in her next request.
Raymond, help me count them.

They waded through these small deaths with rubber gloves,
listened to the thump of each dead rat as it rustled against
the slackness of plastic bags.
Raymond wanted to stop counting,
but mama needed to save a dozen dollars
wherever she could
if they wanted to finally leave the rats behind.

After the last rat was counted, Raymond handed
the bag to the landlord as proof. *Here.*

Enough rats to skip the rent for three months.
Enough rats to avoid the fear of sweet sleeping
breath leading to bitten lips.
Healthy children wrapped in designer dictates
cannot describe Raymond's fear of rabies,
the smell of poison rotting from the inside out,
the scratching inside the walls at night.

Those children
should find soft lives
that drop pendulums in their dreams
and never tell another story
about the ghetto
until they've had to count rats
with their hands.

Postcard to an Ecologist

Last year
I heard tell
a striped snake
crossed the sandy road
where grandma lives.

Walking
the humid farm today,
I saw that striped snake
crossing the sandy road
where grandma lives.

And when tomorrow comes,
I will wait with my garden hoe
for that striped snake
who crosses the sandy road
where grandma lives.

Nature Boy

Air over the place partially occupied by crows going places every evening;
the extent unseen from sidewalk or porch but obvious, because of the noise,
even from a distance. Noise glosses—harsh, shrill, a wild card. Sundown's a
place for the eye, crows alongside that. Talk's a rough ride, to me, what with
the temptation to out-talk. At best long term memory's the same cranky
argument—changeless, not a tête-à-tête—over distance: to me, the category
animals excludes birds, the plain-jane ones and birds of passage, both. To
me, song's even more ambiguous—chant itself, the place of connection
and association. It's birdless, bereft. I'm impartial, anhedonic. I'm lucky
about distance but I would be remiss if I didn't hesitate over image before
going on.

ROBERT HAYDEN

A Plague of Starlings

invasive bird species brought from Europe →

Fisk Campus — HBC

Evenings I hear
the workmen fire
into the stiff
magnolia leaves,
routing the starlings
gathered noisy and
befouling there.

walking accross campus seeing all these dead black starlings

Their scissoring
terror like glass
coins spilling breaking
the birds explode
into mica sky
raggedly fall
to ground rigid
in clench of cold.

The spared return,
when the guns are through,
to the spoiled trees
like choiceless poor
to a dangerous
dwelling place,
chitter and quarrel
in the piercing dark
above the killed.

killing of birds - seen as nusance

Mornings, I pick
my way past death's
black droppings: → *the birds or*
on campus lawns   *non-humans of nature*
and streets
the troublesome
starlings
frost-salted lie,
troublesome still.

And if not careful
I shall tread
upon carcasses
carcasses when I
go mornings now
to lecture on
what Socrates,
the hemlock hour nigh,
told sorrowing
Phaedo and the rest
about the migratory
habits of the soul.

O Believer

Bridal veil, lilies, catnip, rose—
beneath a pin oak tree a yella woman
rakes leaves and bracken as a snake unpeels
itself, slow, unwinding down above her head,
and the yella woman feels that long black reaching
and runs screaming, *Snake! Snake!*

And the colored children come, curious,
and her own brown babies watch
as a big boy comes to shoot it with his rifle,
missing and missing and missing until
finally the snake drops, hanging
for a moment like a question, a tongue
about to speak and deciding: not.

Some liquid part of the tree unwound,
each leaf made serpent, reptilian bark coiling
into roots. He takes it away, the big boy, takes the snake
to a ditch, or maybe he goes with it from house
to house to show: the snake that scared the yella woman.

O believer, Sistah Eve
wasn't tempted by no snake—but by that tree,
a tree showing its true nature: wanting,
and wanting God's attention to itself.
It was the tree that tempted her and not the snake.

The snake hung suspended over
a yella woman's head, over her yolk-skin, wanting
only to swallow her, or to lie against her skin, warm.

And her brown babies stand on one leg,
scratching behind one knee with the other foot,
watching their mama and this danger. Only
her oldest will remember, will hold the molted
skin of this memory: a snake molasses-winding
from a pin oak tree, understanding about temptation
and longing, how it is dark and sweet, how it hangs
over us, quietly watching, drawing closer.

The Brown Menace or Poem to the Survival of Roaches

Call me
your deepest urge
toward survival
call me
and my brothers and sisters
in the sharp smell of your refusal
call me
roach and presumptious
nightmare on your white pillow
your itch to destroy
the indestructible
part of yourself.

Call me
your own determination
in the most detestable shape
you can become
friend of your image
within me   compares to roach
I am you
in your most deeply cherished nightmare
scuttling through the painted cracks
you create to admit me
into your kitchens
into your fearful midnights
into your values at noon
in your most secret places
with hate
you learn to honor me
by imitation

as I alter—
through your greedy preoccupations
through your kitchen wars
and your poisonous refusal—
to survive.

To survive.

Survive.

strength of roach
↳ is it intentional,
does it want to
live?

how is the man the
roach?   or woman

KWAME ALEXANDER

Life

for Professor Derrick Bell

This morning
I woke to find
termites
eating away
at my home . . .
my friends
assured me that
the good
liberal ones
were not involved

What a Snakehead Discovered in a Maryland Pond and a Poet in Corporate America Have in Common

The snakehead is a voracious fish from China's Yangtze River. It can breathe air and "walk" on land—able to crawl out of the water and survive for up to three days while searching for a new body of water if necessary. These critters could devastate the native ecosystem and be almost impossible to control.
—James A. Swan

My fins are foreign, my gills versatile
because they've always had to be.
Despite alleged aggression,
I cut these teeth for protection.

You understand how the others swim,
but me—my travel mystifies,
terrifies a little.
You figure if you don't "get" me,
I'll somehow get you good—
invading and transforming the habitat forever.

How do you do what you do?
Where are you coming from?
How should I manage you?

I propelled myself upon rugged land
to reach this pond,
buried in the muddy bottom for years.
Both of us marvel
that I've survived this long undetected.

Keep your poisons, your devious nets,
whatever ridding you have in mind.
There is no need to slice and bleed me.
Just because I can, doesn't mean I ever planned
to wipe you out.

I've heaved my greatness before.
I'll do it again,
back to incredible, exotic waters in which
you would drown.

The Lost Conquistador

A breeze beginning. Black, unshining flake
in shifting screens—these chopped in trees,
continually, then scattered loose,
no, not loose (note the small dance) then
shattered with their tethers hidden
still somehow attached—the flake
grounded now
       now moving (A beetle. A flying ant. A beetle.) along the sand path
among pieces of light and
in sudden wind:
        the glance in grass
the glance in swung around
           darkness
a dance of particulates, then a shifting
(bird wings beating water)
a coalescing . . .
         Refocus:
beetle at the green edge
(have I seen anything?)
         others no doubt
down there. Fidelity.
In extreme. In
the green wires sprung
from earth to meet his legs
the stutter
in each blade, the return
and there
       the dirt's near invisible throwing
moves the glance
past tiny piled stones (little basilicas)

pinning what
slew, what shut motive
beneath them,
bulking some unseeable gathering, impossible to—
and what besides sand—the thinnest particulars—builds itself
impregnable grammar . . .

The beetle is not a messenger. I can see that.
He grows into things.
              The light around him. For example.

Is the fuse point of his leaving.
Is the clawing in the center.
Claimed by anything?
The focus.
          Is it claimed?: (Twig as bridge,
                              leaf shard as scrap of night)

And after the sunlight killings of small scenes,
the greying out.
And whose idea of a place in the vibrant guttural repose of an antlered
    thing . . .

Step
around to the green now
of where he might be
going.
Everything to
not lay a hand in his path.
Everything to
not smooth it over.
(What shall I do for my birthday?)
It might be
he stops
in patterns of sunlight
            a half step farther out,
it might be some loosening . . .

Lapse.
Location.
Lapse.

Comes now,
        burnished,
                a perfect translation of—a hiving out
of air
some small tar
intensity.
        Comes,
irreducible pinprick
            choosing through
                    delicate green steeples.
Serious selector,
            how to distinguish (how to hurt)
A breeze beginning.
I lie on my side among the (watch now)
                phalanx guards of green,
        the bare
rigor of a broad mind in its plainness
its refusal to look (how to hurt)
the smile of light
on the shell,
            discrimination of the oblivious dark little hum
ground somehow
in the middle of a long light—
all the others (how to dream)—tendrils
frail legs
supporting
one thing,
        (how to damage)

now a breath hole

now a small turning

now a tiny reddish light

                        stopped

now a clinging eye—

the beginning of the end of the world

cockroach population possibly declining
—news report

maybe the morning the roaches
walked into the kitchen
bold with they bad selves
marching up out of the drains
not like soldiers   like priests
grim and patient in the sink
and when we ran the water
trying to drown them as if they were
soldiers   they seemed to bow their
sad heads   for us not at us
and march single file away

maybe then   the morning we rose
from our beds as always
listening for the bang of the end
of the world   maybe then
when we heard only the tiny tapping
and saw them dark and prayerful
in the kitchen   maybe then
when we watched them turn from us
faithless at last
and walk in a long line away

[handwritten annotations:]
→ spacing, ties in religion

→ reality of future
- whats causing the end?
- sense of divide & misunderstanding of one another

Carpenter Bee

All winter long I have passed
beneath her nest—a hole no bigger
than the tip of my thumb.

Last year, before I was here,
she burrowed into the wood
framing my porch, drilled a network

[handwritten: way she referenes the bee]

of tunnels, her round body sturdy
for the work of building. Torpid
the cold months, she now pulls herself

[handwritten: how does this relate to enslaved people]

out into the first warm days of spring
to tread the air outside my screen door,
floating in pure sunlight, humming

against a backdrop of green. She too
must smell the wisteria, see
—with her hundred eyes—purple

[handwritten: purple]

blossoms lacing the trees. Flower-
hopping, she draws invisible lines,
the geometry of her flight. Drunk

on nectar, she can still find her way
back; though now, she must be
confused, disoriented, doubting even

her own homing instinct—this beeline,
now, to nowhere. Today, the workmen
have come, plugged the hole—her threshold—

covered it with thick white paint, a scent
acrid and unfamiliar. She keeps hovering,
buzzing around the spot. Watching her,

I think of what I've left behind, returned to,
only to find everything changed, nothing but
my memory intact—like her eggs, still inside,

each in its separate cell—snug, ordered, certain.

Yellowjackets

When the plowblade struck
An old stump hiding under
The soil like a beggar's
Rotten tooth, they swarmed up
& Mister Jackson left the plow
Wedged like a whaler's harpoon.
The horse was midnight
Against dusk, tethered to somebody's
Pocketwatch. He shivered, but not
The way women shook their heads
Before mirrors at the five
& dime—a deeper connection
To the low field's evening star.
He stood there, in tracechains,
Lathered in froth, just
Stopped by a great, goofy
Calmness. He whinnied
Once, & then the whole
Beautiful, blue-black sky
Fell on his back.

Forsaken of the Earth

The Flowers

It seemed to Myop as she skipped lightly from hen house to pigpen to smoke-house that the days had never been as beautiful as these. The air held a keen-ness that made her nose twitch. The harvesting of the corn and cotton, pea-nuts and squash, made each day a golden surprise that caused excited little tremors to run up her jaws.

Myop carried a short, knobby stick. She struck out at random at chickens she liked, and worked out the beat of a song on the fence around the pigpen. She felt light and good in the warm sun. She was ten, and nothing existed for her but her song, the stick clutched in her dark brown hand, and the tat-de-ta-ta-ta of accompaniment.

Turning her back on the rusty boards of her family's sharecropper cabin, Myop walked along the fence till it ran into the stream made by the spring. Around the spring, where the family got drinking water, silver ferns and wild-flowers grew. Along the shallow banks pigs rooted. Myop watched the tiny white bubbles disrupt the thin black scale of soil and the water that silently rose and slid away down the stream.

She had explored the woods behind the house many times. Often, in late autumn, her mother took her to gather nuts among the fallen leaves. Today she made her own path, bouncing this way and that way, vaguely keeping an eye out for snakes. She found, in addition to various common but pretty ferns and leaves, an armful of strange blue flowers with velvety ridges and a sweet suds bush full of the brown, fragrant buds.

By twelve o'clock, her arms laden with sprigs of her findings, she was a mile or more from home. She had often been as far before, but the strangeness of the land made it not as pleasant as her usual haunts. It seemed gloomy in the little cove in which she found herself. The air was damp, the silence close and deep.

Myop began to circle back to the house, back to the peacefulness of the morning. It was then she stepped smack into his eyes. Her heel became lodged in the broken ridge between brow and nose, and she reached down quickly, unafraid, to free herself. It was only when she saw his naked grin that she gave a little yelp of surprise.

He had been a tall man. From feet to neck covered a long space. His head lay beside him. When she pushed back the leaves and layers of earth and debris Myop saw that he'd had large white teeth, all of them cracked or broken, long fingers, and very big bones. All his clothes had rotted away except some threads of blue denim from his overalls. The buckles of the overalls had turned green.

Myop gazed around the spot with interest. Very near where she'd stepped into the head was a wild pink rose. As she picked it to add to her bundle she noticed a raised mound, a ring, around the rose's root. It was the rotted remains of a noose, a bit of shredding plowline, now blending benignly into the soil. Around an overhanging limb of a great spreading oak clung another piece. Frayed, rotted, bleached, and frazzled—barely there—but spinning restlessly in the breeze. Myop laid down her flowers.

And the summer was over.

PHILLIS WHEATLEY

On Imagination

Thy various works, imperial queen, we see,
How bright their forms! how deck'd with pomp by thee!
Thy wond'rous acts in beauteous order stand,
And all attest how potent is thine hand.
From *Helicon's* refulgent heights attend,
Ye sacred choir, and my attempts befriend:
To tell her glories with a faithful tongue,
Ye blooming graces, triumph in my song.
Now here, now there, the roving *Fancy* flies,
Till some lov'd objects strikes her wand'ring eyes,
Whose silken fetters all the senses bind,
And soft captivity involves the mind.

in love, secret

Imagination! who can sing thy force?
Or who describe the swiftness of thy course?
Soaring though air to find the bright abode,
Th' empyreal palace of the thund'ring God,
We on thy pinions can surpass the wind,
And leave the rolling universe behind;
From star to star the mental optics rove,
Measure the skies, and range the realms above.
There in one view we grasp the mighty whole,
Or with new worlds amaze th' unbounded soul.

Though *winter* frowns to *Fancy's* raptur'd eyes
The fields may flourish, and gay scenes arise;
The frozen deeps may break their iron bands,
And bid their waters murmur o'er the sands.
Fair *Flora* may resume her fragrant reign,
And with her flow'ry riches deck the plain;

nature

149

Sylvanus may diffuse his honours round,
And all the forest may with leaves be crown'd;
Show'rs may descend, and dews their gems disclose,
And nectar sparkle on the blooming rose.

Such is thy pow'r, nor are thine orders vain,
O thou the leader of the mental train:
In full perfection all thy works are wrought,
And thine the sceptre o'er the realms of thought.
Before thy throne the subject-passions bow,
Of subject-passions sov'reign ruler Thou,
At thy command joy rushes on the heart,
And through the glowing veins the spirits dart.

Fancy might now her silken pinions try
To rise from earth, and sweep th' expanse on high;
From *Tithon's* bed now might *Aurora* rise,
Her cheeks all glowing with celestial dies,
While a pure stream of light o'erflows the skies.
The monarch of the day I might behold,
And all the mountains tipt with radiant gold,
But I reluctant leave the pleasing views,
Which *Fancy* dresses to delight the *Muse*;
Winter austere forbids me to aspire,
And northern tempests damp the rising fire;
They chill the tides of *Fancy's* flowing sea,
Cease then, my song, cease the unequal lay.

[Handwritten annotations:]

wood, forest — Roman God of Forests

→ nature (forest)

Use of fancy throughout

latin, Aurora, dawn — Roman Goddess of sunrise

Greek son of Laomedon & a lover of Eos ↓ immortality for him but not eternal youth

('unequal lay')

150

For Saundra

i wanted to write
a poem
that rhymes
but revolution doesn't lend
itself to be-bopping

then my neighbor
who thinks i hate
asked—do you ever write
tree poems—i like trees
so i thought
i'll write a beautiful green tree poem
peeked from my window
to check the image
noticed that the school yard was covered
with asphalt
no green—no trees grow
in manhattan

then, well, i thought the sky
i'll do a big blue sky poem
but all the clouds have winged
low since no-Dick was elected

so i thought again
and it occurred to me
maybe i shouldn't write
at all

but clean my gun
and check my kerosene supply

perhaps these are not poetic
times
at all

The Natural World

You got trees all dappled with sunlight and shit
You got trees green with lots of leaves
You got fruit-bearing trees   made for climbing
          good for something

I got trees too   My trees stainless steel poles
with no flags   My trees streetlights redyellowgreen
glass shattered on the ground

You got birds waking you up in the morning
Birds waking you up the morning   TweetTweet
ChirpChirp   That's how it is for y'all
                              mutherfuckers

I got birds too   My birds
loud as jackhammers   My birds
loud as police sirens   My birds
loud as gunfire   My birds
electric   gas-powered

My birds   My birds   killers

Lament for Dark Peoples

I was a red man one time,
But the white men came.
I was a black man, too,
But the white men came.

They drove me out of the forest.
They took me away from the jungles.
I lost my trees.
I lost my silver moons.

Now they've caged me
In the circus of civilization.
Now I herd with the many—
Caged in the circus of civilization.

White Things

Most things are colorful things—the sky, earth, and sea.
       Black men are most men; but the white are free!
White things are rare things; so rare, so rare
They stole from out a silvered world—somewhere.
Finding earth-plains fair plains, save greenly grassed,
They strewed white feathers of cowardice, as they passed;
       The golden stars with lances fine
       The hills all red and darkened pine,
They blanched with their wand of power;
And turned the blood in a ruby rose
To a poor white poppy-flower.

They pyred a race of black, black men,
And burned them to ashes white; then,
Laughing, a young one claimed a skull,
For the skull of a black is white, not dull,
       But a glistening awful thing;
       Made, it seems, for this ghoul to swing
In the face of God with all his might,
And swear by the hell that siréd him:
       "Man-maker, make white!"

think Black ethos in American south

Parsley

1. The Cane Fields

There is a parrot imitating spring
in the palace, its feathers parsley green.
Out of the swamp the cane appears

to haunt us, and we cut it down. El General
searches for a word; he is all the world
there is. Like a parrot imitating spring,

we lie down screaming as rain punches through
and we come up green. We cannot speak an R—
out of the swamp, the cane appears

and then the mountain we call in whispers *Katalina*.
The children gnaw their teeth to arrowheads.
There is a parrot imitating spring.

El General has found his word: *perejil.*
Who says it, lives. He laughs, teeth shining
out of the swamp. The cane appears

in our dreams, lashed by wind and streaming.
And we lie down. For every drop of blood
there is a parrot imitating spring.
Out of the swamp the cane appears.

2. The Palace

The word the general's chosen is parsley.
It is fall, when thoughts turn
to love and death; the general thinks

of his mother, how she died in the fall
and he planted her walking cane at the grave
and it flowered, each spring stolidly forming
four-star blossoms. The general

pulls on his boots, he stomps to
her room in the palace, the one without
curtains, the one with a parrot
in a brass ring. As he paces he wonders
Who can I kill today. And for a moment
the little knot of screams
is still. The parrot, who has traveled

all the way from Australia in an ivory
cage, is, coy as a widow, practicing
spring. Ever since the morning
his mother collapsed in the kitchen
while baking skull-shaped candies
for the Day of the Dead, the general
has hated sweets. He orders pastries
brought up for the bird; they arrive

dusted with sugar on a bed of lace.
The knot in his throat starts to twitch;
he sees his boots the first day in battle
splashed with mud and urine
as a soldier falls at his feet amazed—
how stupid he looked!—at the sound
of artillery. *I never thought it would sing*
the soldier said, and died. Now

the general sees the fields of sugar   *after death*
cane, lashed by rain and streaming.
He sees his mother's smile, the teeth
gnawed to arrowheads. He hears
the Haitians sing without R's
as they swing the great machetes:
Katalina, they sing, *Katalina,*

mi madle, mi amol en muelte. God knows
his mother was no stupid woman; she
could roll an R like a queen. Even
a parrot can roll an R! In the bare room
the bright feathers arch in a parody
of greenery, as the last pale crumbs
disappear under the blackened tongue. Someone

calls out his name in a voice
so like his mother's, a startled tear
splashes the tip of his right boot.
My mother, my love in death.
The general remembers the tiny green sprigs
men of his village wore in their capes
to honor the birth of a son. He will
order many, this time, to be killed

for a single, beautiful word.

The Haunted Oak

Pray why are you so bare, so bare,
    Oh, bough of the old oak-tree;
And why, when I go through the shade you throw,
    Runs a shudder over me?

My leaves were green as the best, I trow,
    And sap ran free in my veins,
But I saw in the moonlight dim and weird
    A guiltless victim's pains.

I bent me down to hear his sigh;
    I shook with his gurgling moan,
And I trembled sore when they rode away,
    And left him here alone.

They'd charged him with the old, old crime,
    And set him fast in jail:
Oh, why does the dog howl all night long,
    And why does the night wind wail?

He prayed his prayer and he swore his oath,
    And he raised his hand to the sky;
But the beat of hoofs smote on his ear,
    And the steady tread drew nigh.

Who is it rides by night, by night,
    Over the moonlit road?
And what is the spur that keeps the pace,
    What is the galling goad?

And now they beat at the prison door,
    "Ho, keeper, do not stay!
We are friends of him whom you hold within,
    And we fain would take him away

From those who ride fast on our heels
    With mind to do him wrong;
They have no care for his innocence,
    And the rope they bear is long."

They have fooled the jailer with lying words,
    They have fooled the man with lies;
The bolts unbar, the locks are drawn,
    And the great door open flies.

Now they have taken him from the jail,
    And hard and fast they ride,
And the leader laughs low down in his throat,
    As they halt my trunk beside.

Oh, the judge, he wore a mask of black,
    And the doctor one of white,
And the minister, with his oldest son,
    Was curiously bedight.

Oh, foolish man, why weep you now?
    'Tis but a little space,
And the time will come when these shall dread
    The mem'ry of your face.

I feel the rope against my bark,
    And the weight of him in my grain,
feel in the throe of his final woe
    The touch of my own last pain.

And never more shall leaves come forth
    On the bough that bears the ban;

I am burned with dread, I am dried and dead,
    From the curse of a guiltless man.

And ever the judge rides by, rides by,
    And goes to hunt the deer,
And ever another rides his soul
    In the guise of a mortal fear.

And ever the man he rides me hard,
    And never a night stays he;
For I feel his curse as a haunted bough,
    On the trunk of a haunted tree.

from *Rape of Florida*, Canto I

I

The negro slave by Swanee river sang;
Well-pleased he listened to his echoes ringing;
For in his heart a secret comfort sprang,
When Nature seemed to join his mournful singing.
To mem'ry's cherished objects fondly clinging;
His bosom felt the sunset's patient glow,
And spirit whispers into weird life springing,
Allured to worlds he trusted yet to know,
And lightened for a while life's burdens here below.

II

The drowsy dawn from many a low-built shed,
Beheld his kindred driven to their task;
Late evening saw them turn with weary tread
And painful faces back; and dost thou ask
How sang these bondsmen? how their suff'rings mask?
Song is the soul of sympathy divine,
And hath an inner ray where hope may bask;
Song turns the poorest waters into wine,
Illumines exile hearts and makes their faces shine.

III

The negro slave by Swanee river sang,
There soon the human hunter rode along;
and eagerly behind him came a gang
of hounds and men,—the bondman hushed his song—
Around him came a silent, list'ning throng;
"Some runaway!" he muttered; said no more,

But sank from view the growing corn among;
And though deep pangs his wounded spirit bore,
He hushed his soul, and went on singing as before.

IV

So fared the land where slaves were groaning yet—
Where beauty's eyes must feed the lusts of men!
'Tis as when horrid dreams we half forget,
Would then relate, and still relate again—
Ah! cold abhorrence hesitates my pen!
The heavens were sad, and hearts of men were faint;
Philanthropy implored and wept, but then
The wrong, unblushing trampled on Restraint,
With feeble Law sat by and uttered no complaint.

V

"Fly and be free!" A whisper comes from heaven,
"Thy cries are heard!" the bondman's up and gone!
To grasp the dearest boon to mortals given,
He frantic flies, unaided and alone.
To him the red man's dwellings are unknown;
But he can crave the freedom of his race,
Can find his harvests in the desert sown,
And in the cypress forest's dark embrace
A pathway to his lonely habitations trace.

VI

The sable slave, from Georgia's utmost bounds,
Escapes for life into the Great Wahoo.
Here he has left afar the savage hounds
And human hunters that did late pursue;
There in the hommock darkly hid from view,
His wretched limbs are stretched awhile to rest,
Till some kind Seminole shall guide him thro'
To where by hound nor hunter more distrest,
He, in a flow'ry home, shall be the red man's guest.

VII

If tilled profusion does not crown the view,
Nor wide-ranged farms begirt with fences spread;
The cultivated plot is well to do;
And where no slave his groaning life has led,
The songs of plenty fill the lowliest shed.
Who could wish more, When Nature, always green,
Brings forth fruit-bearing woods and fields of bread?
Wish more, where cheerful valleys bloom between,
And herds browse on the hills, where winter ne'er has been?

. . . .

X

Fair Florida! whose scenes could so enhance—
Could in the sweetness of the earth excel!
Wast thou the Seminole's inheritance?
Yea, it was thee he loved, and loved so well!
'Twas 'neath thy palms and pines he strove to dwell.
Not savage, but resentful to the knife,
For these he sternly struggled—sternly fell!
Thoughtful and brave, in long uneven strife,
He held the verge of manhood mid the heights of life.

XI

A wild-born pride endeared him to thy soil!
When roamed his herds without a keeper's care—
Where man knew not the pangs of slavish toil!
And where thou didst not blooming pleasure spare,
But well allotted each an ample share,
He loved to dwell: Oh! isn't the goal of life
Where man has plenty and to man is fair?
When free from avarice's pinch and strife.
Is earth not like the Eden-home of man and wife?

. . . .

XIX

Oh! sing it in the light of freedom's morn,
Tho' tyrant wars have made the earth a grave;
The good, the great, and true, are, if so, born,
And so with slaves, *chains do not make the slave!*
If high-souled birth be what the mother gave,—
If manly birth, and manly to the core,—
Whate'er the test, the man will he behave!
Crush him to earth and crush him o'er and o'er.
A man he'll rise at last and meet you as before.

DOUGLAS KEARNEY

Swimchant of Nigger Mer-Folk (An Aquaboogie Set in Lapis)

let yo fishbone slip o men / let yo fishbone slip 'omen / let yo fishbone slip o men / let yo fishbone slip 'omen / let yo fishbone slip o men

mako wish
ye black fish
mako feed
be black bleed

hammerheads'
hammers head

to ham (or head?)
til hammers fed

they's comp'ny
comin comin

o they's comp'ny
knockin knockin

grate   white jaw
Aw! great white
jaw-jaw juju
gnaw gnaw   NO! NO...
they's comp'ny
dinin dinin

duppyguppies say
stay we in azure-amber
can't re-member;
c'ant remember
o they's comp'ny
haintin haintin

never learned to swim/but me sho can di've.

O, VERMILION SHIP—D'WAH-WAH-OOO.
OVER MILLIONS SHIPPED. WAH-WAH-OO.

and all about was a darkening cloud and the gullets filled of brine and kine [cattle/chattel]
charnel channel of a deep blue. See
all about that darkening cloud and the gullets full of water and the gullets full of slaughter, [a salt/assault] o
charnel channel of a deep blue sea.

Poseidon slides his foaming shroud assured no one will see.

"Jus look at   de worl aroun you——right ere on   de ocean floor——such wonduhful tings surroun you——what more is you lookin for?"
[so sang a pair of raggit claws/scuttlin cross the flo of silent seas. o, ye nigger mer-folk. A lovesong to songlubbers! It'll all be fin(e)???]

**ATTENTION: NIGGER MERMAIDS, MERMEN & MERNINNIES CHAINED LIKE HOOKED & SINKED SARDINNIES:
DO NOT BLEED IN THE SEA. THE STAINS WON'T WASH OUT. WE AIN'TNT RESPONSIBLE FOR YOUR MESS.**

MUCH OBILGED, THEE MANAGEMENT

{Voyage: through.}

they's comp'ny haintin haintin/can't re-member/c'ant remember/o they's comp'ny haintin haintin/the stains won't wash out

CLARENCE MAJOR

Water USA

america, tom sawyer, is bigger
than your swim
hole. You meant, the union, water-
falls, one waterfall
a path near, from which you
jump, folklore, holding
your nose. a chemical change
takes place as you pollute
the water i drink. as your
jet lands, crashing my
environment. tom sawyer can't hold
all the dead bodies upright
nor get anything
out of a lecture on control
systems. and bigger
thomas didn't have an even
chance to study chemistry

Migration

That summer, municipality was on everyone's lips,
Even the earth eaters who put the pastor in pastoral.
Truth is: my zeal for chicory waned, and my chest was damp.
I shivered by a flagpole, knowing betrayal
Was coming my way. Just the same, I believed like a guitar string
Believes in distance and addressed each bright star
Lord of My Feet. A country of overnight deputies, everyone had a knot
To endeavor. I read oaks and poplars for signs: charred branches,
Tobacco leaves strung up to die, swamp soil in my soul.
Ever trace the outline of a phantom mob, even if you were late arriving?

- Great migration

- what happens to souls when
  they pass away?

- fleaing in fear

RUTH ELLEN KOCHER

February Leaving

There was a thick summer.
There were cicadas and rows of grave markers,
mothers knitting and grandmothers
weaving their fading thoughts into combs of silver hair,
lightning bugs lost and flagging the woods,
homes that whispered to each other at midnight
the truth from their cellars.
I could say that none of this lives in us
because at night there are fewer hands
to wind the air into our pockets,
that bats are nervous in their temporary waking.
I can tell you that the grass sorrows
if there is no thunder or the earth shudders
where people sleep or the mountains mouth
their wishes silently into snow.

The truth is, in winter, the earth rejects us.

What do you say with memory—
that the continents long for each other
just as children who are bundled ghosts
leave their voices as trails in the woods,
that lakes are burdened with notions of ice
and heaviness, just like us.
The things we trust are less
and less true in winter.
I will say only that a cough
deep inside you
at the heart of your lung
will turn you around just in time

to see the rock cliffs you've dreamed of,
the bull seals searching
for beaches, for rocks that hold
the moss long, long into summer,
and a sun that's indifferent to the year,
to the herd, and to the ocean charging.

ED ROBERSON

blue horses

the cold has put blue horses where lambs were.
and quiet cows that fattened in the night
upon the grass are driven in and stones
wild veined with ice have taken over in
the fields: the moon is chewing on the snow.
and something watching from a stand of pines
has tied off screams into a hanging knot

~ owl? "screams"

the road has spent the night of winter clean
of passengers: the thread out of the hills
has helped the naked trees remain in love
on their bare bodies. the decent leaves unmade.
and nothing warm has passed inside the gate
to say a word against the solid well
nor the bucket cord that does not weave its drink.

there is a man who, if he cried, the hard
rare droppings of the wolves digesting hunger
would tear his grunting eyes: who, if he spoke,
the shrill fillings of dead men's teeth could cut
his gums with silences they know, who lives
one valley from the sun, who if he loved—
would simply love and roll from her unnoticed
by her arriving immigrant bees.

Sick Man Looks at Flowers

You are sick and old, and there is a closing in.
The eyes gone dead to all that would entice.

Echoes are dull and the body accepts no touch
Except its pain. Mind is a little isle.

But now invades this audacity of red!
This ripe rebuke, this burgeoning affluence
Mocks me and mocks the desert of my bed.

ARNA BONTEMPS

Prodigal

I shall come back when dogwood flowers are going
And passing drakes are honking toward the south
With eager necks, I shall come back knowing
The old unanswered question on your mouth.

When frost is on the manzonita shoots
And dogwoods at the spring are turning brown,
There between the interlacing roots
With folded arms I shall at last go down.

potters' field

in the throat of crownsville, maryland
       beneath the filament of pine and tobacco
reedy blue asters outline the old prison cottage
for colored women
           held in parch and punishment

                forensics is memory

a sash of light from the monocacy river arcs   BELOVED
      while maddish seasons
dismember   her station hulled beneath the muck   turned livid
on the edges of things like vindictive weeds or nervous trees
      a caste even unto death
      as though bone may copulate
               with bone

NATASHA TRETHEWEY

Monument

Today the ants are busy
       beside my front steps, weaving
in and out of the hill they're building.
       I watch them emerge and—

like everything I've forgotten—disappear
       into the subterranean—a world
made by displacement. In the cemetery
       last June, I circled, lost—

weeds and grass grown up all around—
       the landscape blurred and waving.
At my mother's grave, ants streamed in
       and out like arteries, a tiny hill rising

above her untended plot. Bit by bit,
       red dirt piled up, spread
like a rash on the grass; I watched a long time
       the ants' determined work,

how they brought up soil
       of which she will be part,
and piled it before me. Believe me when I say
       I've tried not to begrudge them

their industry, this reminder of what
       I haven't done. Even now,
the mound is a blister on my heart,
       a red and humming swarm.

Disasters, Natural and Other

Disasters, Nature, and Poetry

Most disasters come suddenly, and leave people with great loss. On any continent, in any country, in any state or town of the American union, a disaster is a Janus-head, a two-faced blow below the belt to the human spirit and sensibility. Any loss is felt deeply, but especially when it touches home, perhaps the excruciating loss of a relative or friend or a first pet. Such personal, individual tragedy shatters us in ways we never thought possible. One day, one moment, we are full of this life; and in the next is emptiness, absence, aching. In the United States alone, in recent years, people have been bombarded with tornadoes, massive fires in neighborhoods and forests, snow storms, wind storms, floods naturally occurring from rains over-soaking lands to unnatural floods such as post-Katrina flooding caused by the failure of the levee system in New Orleans. Such disasters, personal and public, humble the rich, squash the working class and poor, and loom in the creative imagination immortalized for decades to come. Why and how? More than the reports of the thing, more than the various yarns or stories, more than the event itself, through poetry the creative imagination captures the human take on the event or experience as a higher order of consciousness and redelivers the human sensibility, an inner translation of the outer.

In words, from painting the beauty of flowers to recalling disasters, poetry retells by creating a logic all its own in mind and metaphor, in history and memory, in echoes of contemporary events and lines painting loss and awareness of drastic change, in narratives and lyrics, in haiku, blues, sonnets, or other various forms. In any disaster, the life held dear or even just familiar is turned upside down, emptied. This upheaval is more than a staggering shock; it is a decimation. Poetry can reveal the human consciousness in layers and reveal humanity in all its frailty and grandeur.

Black writers began in the cradle of civilization weaving the earliest epics. With moans, hollers, and rhythms, that memory traveled, surviving "middle passage" horrors, and translated into the American landscape only after many uneasy ends, from slavery to jim crow. In those early tenuous days, where men too often dangled from trees like strange fruit, we can be reminded in a poem, written in the persona of a tree, that the memory of these horrors are unnatural disasters which resonate boldly. What does it mean to lose your language, to be forbidden your culture, to be raped from your homeland? Poets take us on a voyage from the past to the present. Poems provide crucial reminders of the holes in our hearts as a people, for us and all humanity. How would we know what happened? How do and did we survive? What happens to us through these natural and unnatural disasters? How can we handle this?

From the earliest epics, such as the Mali epic *Sundiata*, the original lion king, much is made of heroic journeys and superhuman acts; but the most important revelation is a sense of the human spirit, some kind of fortitude, and even that is eclipsed by the original force within all of us to "combat" our fears. Poetry may reveal inner strength on the one hand and human fragility on the other hand. The spirit captured in these tales of heroism continues throughout history, recalling significant travels, the experience of wars, or shipwrecked voyages. For example, in the African American literary tradition, from the oral folk poetry to spirituals, to a substantial amount of contemporary works, there is often grand celebration or singing of sorts, from the likes of ancient bards to contemporary rappers; but often lurking beneath singing is fear. This fear is full of racial memory, with echoes of that fated "middle passage" across the Atlantic from Africa to the New World, when families torn apart were tossed on strange waters; this disaster is a haunting of hate, a strong undercurrent that rises through centuries to human beings intimate with fear in a continual state of "hostile waters." These are the black people of all of America and the diaspora. Such poetry reflects the wages of fear and hate; and in that retelling, something magnificent happens, a recognition of the sorrow and angst that allows a possible healing.

From historical disasters to contemporary ones, what was is shaken from the ground up. How does one weather an earthquake? We watch the nightly news in disbelief attempting to process the rubble, the hundreds of thousands lost in China. How can one capture shock, fear of loss, and the awe in a nature creating chaos that shakes belief in reality and staggers moments with fear? Poetry. Poetry can unseat catastrophe with comic relief in a stark rendering of a horror so natural and so overwhelming only the story of it reminds us of our vulnerability and ability to continue. Whether the disaster is recent or not, picture burning neighborhoods, wildfires in California, everything smoldering and burned to ashes, like clear-cutting cane fields in preparation for tilling. Catastrophes, such as the collapse of the interstate highway during an earthquake, these natural and unnatural disasters, leave deaths, missing people, the interruption of such basic services as communication, travel, food, water, and people hurt, moaning. Journalists can report these events, but poetry vividly narrates the unsteady reality; disaster brings, literally and figuratively, shaky ground.

Poems can depict the impermanence of life, yet imbedded within that impermanence is renewal. Within the original ancient haiku and more contemporary haiku, readers can follow insects through blossoms, and we become aware that an ant or a bee must move on to the next flower, the next experience. Life is a continual motion of love and loss. There is the life cycle: first life, then death, then life again. A moth may struggle against the glow and draw of light, against grains of sand, to become half-burned or half-buried, the insect facing obliteration. Nature and humankind exist in an uneasy peace. This idea is especially driven home in poems that depict the natural magnificence of a deer eating the neighborhood blossoms or coyotes who devour small domestic pets like cats or dogs in a yard. This is taken as more than blasphemy, an illegal impingement. This natural order, the beauty of natural creations, is divorced by urban sprawl and the great American suburban homelands, and only poetry can eloquently express such self-righteous anger and awe.

Other disasters are personal and public. Take the effect of AIDS, a disaster of major proportions devastating families and communities around the world from Africa to America. AIDS has moved from eliminating "hard-bodied men" to erasing generations of young women and their children. Network reporting of the rising numbers of dead and ill is stark and shocking, but poetry juxtaposes Africa's or the San Francisco Bay area's beauty against men and women dying but not giving up. Poetry reminds us of this challenge and difficulty and gives us hope filled with caring and love.

As a black writer, I came to study my craft after a personal disaster. I was crushed in an auto accident six months after marrying very young. For one year, I had no memory; I remembered being married but not my husband; we grew apart. I wrote to remember, to remember my family, my culture, my values, what I hold dear, what I celebrate, what I mourn, for what I long. Who was I? This was a difficult process made palatable by poetry, mostly the poems of black writers: Colleen McElroy—my mentor—Ishmael Reed, Sonia Sanchez, Amiri Baraka, Haki Madhubuti, Carolyn M. Rodgers, Al Young, Audre Lorde, Gwendolyn Brooks, Langston Hughes, then, later, African poets, Native American poets, Irish poets, in whose verse I heard some semblance and the struggle of myself, the sounds of my sweetness and anger. Poetry eased the emptiness I felt and gave me back my humanity. Poetry provided a transmutation for me: I married my culture and values to language, my story to verse. Poetry saved my life, allowed me to heal and become the person I am today.

Later, I wrote to speak for those who can't or won't, those voices of folk who resonate in my head, the stories from my South, my block, the wise and foolish from whom I've fashioned my aesthetic. These years later, reflecting on post-Katrina devastation, this feels like coming full circle; and the disaster is so big, again, I struggle to capture my natural world, my culture, my home. Three weeks after Katrina swept past New Orleans, I returned home hoping my 100-year-old, working-class, modest shotgun family home was standing erect. There was no sign of the voluminous oleanders from beet-red to pale pink, not one azalea bush leaf, only the once great magnolia trees dead in lumps like the various kinds of grass and other vegetation. The once stately majestic oak trees dented and broken. It smelled like carcasses. In this place of semitropics, there was no sound, not a bee, not a mosquito in 85-degree heat. My neighborhood in particular was peopled with families, school kids playing instruments on the way home, or high school bands practicing in the park. No music, no voices, no people, only dead neighborhoods, broken houses, or houses floated off foundations, only silence. It was antilife. My house drowned; and in my library, I lost my unpublished research and over five thousand books, a lifetime of reading and collecting folklore, poetry, fiction, dramas, dictionaries in various languages, reference works on slang and literary history, art books of photography, sculpture, paintings, artistic movements. My lifeline was a blur of text messages from family, friends, and poets concerned for me, sending me quotes of hope and helpfulness. Poetry equals thoughts in motion and order over chaos. Again, poetry, like love, saves me.

The shock continues; there is so much loss of family, home, and the familiar. For most, it is not even our houses, cars, furniture, even if handed down from generations. The magnitude of this disaster is impossible to catalog. What is left in many neighborhoods are steps to homes that once were, or the bare vestiges of a foundation to a home that drowned and collapsed or had to be demolished for safety, far too many blank spaces. What is left are holes in our neighborhoods, holes in our hearts, and a vast interruption in our lives. Those survivors who were torn from their homes or were forced to climb high for dear life and stranded on rooftops will relive that nightmare forever. So many of us lost relatives, friends, neighbors who were extended family for generations. Our names go back centuries. In New Orleans, we are a place of families linked by tradition, and those traditions allow us to continue with some sanity. If we allow ourselves to grieve, we may survive to go on again. If we do not grieve, or do not acknowledge the need to grieve, that loss and disappointment may linger and haunt us, causing its own disasters. What language can capture such loss of power and presence? What form can include such shock? What images can paint such a history? Poetry. Poetry allows us to relive these natural and unnatural disasters and let go, sometimes with humor, sometimes with a profound sense of understanding that only a trope can capture, only a complex of awareness and experience wrapped in language that paints stories. These poems are what is left when dreams die, when worry ripples in waves, when life goes on, and all that is natural fades to be reborn.

Poetry for me has been like early biology lessons of the salamander. We've heard much lately about stem-cell research that may enable regeneration of human tissue. Such miracles have occurred in nature since the very beginning in the salamander. Salamanders, lizards, and other such creatures have the ability to regenerate limbs and other body parts. Actually, humans can as well. The very young can regrow a fingertip. Since I'm not a biologist, please do not ask me to define the process; but in de-differentiation, the cells become more like basic stem cells and can relearn what they need to regrow a fingertip. It is no wonder scientists are preoccupied with the possibilities of stem-cell research. My point here is regeneration, the human ability to start again after loss and trauma, to regrow, relearn, relive a good life. Through poetry, we don't have to wait for scientists.

Through poetry, human beings can relive trauma, injury, catastrophe, whether it is physical, mental, or emotional, real or imagined, and reacquaint ourselves with our most inner resources, our ability to regenerate and manifest as whole again. Through poetry, we can better process our reactions to events, especially disasters, in the world, and react with a higher order of awareness. We don't have to know what it takes to arrive at this new place, for poetry will assist us on our journey and deposit us safely, sometimes uncomfortably, in a new personal place of understanding. We can agree or disagree; we can remain in shallow waters or dive deeply. Through the experience in poetry, our inner vision is awakened.

It is through verse that we make some sense of our world. Poets are not journalists snapping photos. Poetry weaves words to record not just what happens but what sense we can make of it, what is important for us to consider, what is good for us to keep.

ASKIA M. TOURÉ

Floodtide

for the black tenant farmers of the South

"They carry on.
though sorrows completely
bend them down.
they carry on.
though butchered
and maimed
by nature and whitefolks,
they carry on
and sing their songs."

1
drought,
the river is a tricklin' stream.
drought,
dust on the dry tongues
of livestock.
drought,
tobacco leaves
droopin' in the merciless
sunlight.
clear skies, hot and dry.
haze on green mountains.
dustdevils
scamper on the blazin' wind
drought.

nature
non human

(lawd,
we pray for warm soft rain;
for moisture in the fields,
for fat cattle.
lawd,
heah our prayer; rid us
of dis dry spell,
dis merciless heatspell
dis drought.)

] vernacular

2
black clouds on the horizon.
<u>black clouds over green mountains</u>,
lightnin' on the hills.
baaroom, baaroom,
the rumblin' of thunder,
fills the air,
shakes the ground;
it comes:
lightnin' and thunder,
flash and crash;
it comes:
the violent spatter
of burstin'
clouds.

the rain comes
and washes the green mountains;
floods the cotton land.
the rain comes,
ruins the tobacco,
kills the livestock; makin' a mock'ry
of our prayers
for rain.
the killer rain comes:
the river is a ragin' madman.
the river breaks our hearts.

the killer rain comes:
the river takes our shack away.
the river breaks our hearts.
the rain;
the drippin', flooded fields.
the rain;
the dead livestock.
the rain;
the rumblin' of thunder,
the green mountains,
the ragin' river,
the shack;
the killer rain,
the rain.
the killer rain,
the rain.
the killer rain.

3
silence;
gray mist and heartache,
the flooded land.
now, screams; now, cries of rage.
the wails of women
and children,
the cursin' men.
wetsmells, *deathsmells*
of cattle, pigs,
of bloated men,
of hope,
of fallen dreams.

(lawd,
why did yuh cuss us
wit yo' anger?
why did yuh take mah man away?

mah henry,
mah man,
oh lawd!)

churchbells,
the chirpin' of blackbirds,
the sunday air.
sunlight on the flooded fields,   funeral
black throngs gathered,
flowers,
tears for brother henry
and others.   sunday ⟶ Monday

4
monday,
the rooster sounds
his horn:
wake up and live;
cleanup
the flooded land,
the fallen trees, the fields.
rebuild
the shattered homes,
the shattered lives,
the hopes.
rebuild
your shattered dreams.

"though sorrows completely
bend them down.
though butchered and maimed
by nature and whitefolks,   relationship between
they sing their songs,   natur & whitefolk
they sing their songs,   ⟶ now they impact
they sing their songs,   the enslaved
and carry on."

Children of the Mississippi

These know fear; for all their singing
As the moon thrust her tip above dark woods,
Tuning their voices to the summer night,
These folk knew even then the hints of fear.
For all their loafing on the levee,
Unperturbedly spendthrift of time,
Greeting the big boat swinging the curve
"Do it, Mister Pilot! Do it, Big Boy!" *mockery*
Beneath their dark laughter
Roaring like a flood roars, swung into a spillwater,
There rolled even then a strong undertow
Of fear.

Now, intimately
These folk know fear.
They have seen
Blackwater creeping, slow-footed Fate,
Implacably, unceasingly
Over their bottomlands, over their cornshocks,
Past highwater marks, past wildest conjecture,
Black water creeping before their eyes,
Rolling while they toss in startled half sleep.

> De Lord tole Norah
> Dat de flood was due,
> Norah listened to the Lord
> An' got his stock on board,
> Wish dat de Lord
> Had tole us too.

These folk know grief.
They have seen
Black water gurgling, lapping, roaring,
Take their lives' earnings, roll off their paltry
Fixtures of home, things as dear as old hearthgods.
These have known death
Surprising, rapacious of cattle, of children,
Creeping with the black water
Secretly, unceasingly.

> *Death pick out new ways*
> *Now fo' to come to us,*
> *Black water creepin'*
> *While folks is sleepin'*
> *Death on de black water*
> *Ugly an' treacherous.*

black water ~death

These, for all their vaunted faith, know doubt.
These know no Ararat;
No arc of promise bedecking blue skies;
No dove, betokening calm;
No fondled favor towards new beginnings.
These know
Promise of baked lands, burnt as in brickkilns,
Cracked uglily, crinkled crust at seedtime,
Rotten with stench, watched over by vultures.

"vultures"

Promise of winter, bleak and unpitying,
No buoyant hoping now, only dank memories
Bitter as the waters, bracken as the waters,
Black and unceasing as hostile waters.

> *Winter a-comin'*
> *Leaner dan ever,*
> *What we done done to you*
> *Makes you do lak you do?*
> *How we done harmed you*
> *Black-hearted river?*

These folk know fear, now, as bosom crony;
Children, stepchildren → *generational*
Of the Mississippi . . .   *trauma*

Emmett Till

I hear a whistling
Through the water.
Little Emmett
Won't be still.
He keeps floating
Round the darkness,
Edging through
The silent chill.
Tell me, please,
That bedtime story
Of the fairy
River Boy
Who swims forever,
Deep in treasures,
Necklaced in
A coral toy.

sign post

colored water
quarter water
purple water
sugar

still water
deep water
salt water
river

clear water
ice water
rain water
hailing

break water
hard water
white water
drown

Song

The wild trees have bought me
and will sell you a wind
in the forest of falsehoods
where your search must not end

for their roots are not wise.
Strip our loving of dream
pay its secret to thunder
and ransom me home.

Beware oaks in laughter
know hemlock is lying
when she sings of defiance.
The sand words she is saying

will sift over and bury
while the pale moons I hate
seduce you in phases
through oceans of light.

And the wild trees shall sell me
for their safety from lightning
to sand that will flay me
for the next evening's planting.

They will fill my limp skin
with wild dreams from their root
and grow from my flesh
new handfuls of hate

till our ransom is wasted
and the morning speaks out
in a thin voice of wisdom
that loves me too late.

The Sacred History of the Earth

The larkspur blossoms
know when they open themselves
the bee will not stay

A Greenness Taller Than Gods

When we stop,
a green snake starts again
through deep branches.
Spiders mend webs we marched into.
Monkeys jabber in flame trees,
dancing on the limbs to make
fire-colored petals fall. Torch birds
burn through the dark-green day.
The lieutenant puts on sunglasses
& points to an X circled
on his map. When will we learn
to move like trees move?
The point man raises his hand *Wait!*
We've just crossed paths with vc,
branches left quivering.
The lieutenant's right hand says what to do.
We walk into a clearing that blinds.
We move like a platoon of silhouettes
balancing sledge hammers on our heads,
unaware our shadows have untied
from us, wandered off
& gotten lost.

San Francisco, Spring 1986

I feel so East Coast. Shut down, frantic.
Too used to the expensive, the hot-house flowers sold on
every corner. Here the flowers brighten every corner. Free.
Here, the wildflowers are different. Calla lilies grow wild?
Silky, white, trumpet-shaped, composed,

as is this midday light.
Translucent in the Embarcadero.
White, hot, harsh in the Mission.
There, the pink, gray and yellow stucco houses
shutter themselves against the brutal splendor.

As I and Roberto sip beer and talk poetry, politics, the growing list
of men with AIDS, heat is almost forgotten in the midday darkness
of this Salvadoran restaurant.
We patrons linger over plates of rice and beans, vivid spices
harry our hunger as the beers splash down our throats.

This cool seems dreamlike.
Our meal timeless.
But time does matter.

Men, lovers, friends, are
learning women's work.
The weary labor of mothers, sisters, aunts.

How many pills?
Can we afford this?
Here's the doctor's private number.

All the statements that pave the way
for rest, guilt and more work
with someone else.

Here's where the caring begins. Here's where
the caring works. Even as lovers defiantly declare,

"I know he's dying. I won't get tested.
Not just yet."

Here's where the time is taken.
Here's where the story matters.
Where the weeping and the anger
commence.

As if the hard-bodied men
so very young in the Castro,
enterprising in the Haight,
discreet in the Mission
compose an army fighting blind.

And who could be blind to this city's beauty?
Where century-old eucalyptus rend
cathedrals before stone and the sun's lush glow
halos the rise and fall of exhausted hills.

What is so easily available here—the green coast
and an ocean at war with its name—is not so easily
taken away.
These men dying are not given up without love,
without caring, without a fight.

The Cure

The tree stood dying—dying slowly, in the usual manner
of trees, slowly, but not without its clusters of spring leaves
taking shape again, already. The limbs that held them tossed,

shifted, the light fell as it does, through them, though it
sometimes looked as if the light were being shaken, as if
by the branches—the light, like leaves, had it been autumn,

scattering down: singly, in fistfuls. Nothing about it to do
with happiness, or glamour. Not sadness either. That much
I could see, finally. I could see, and want to see. The tree

was itself, its branches were branches, shaking, they shook
in the wind like possibility, like impatient escorts bored with
their own restlessness, like hooves in the wake of desire, in

the wake of the dream of it, and like the branches they were.
A sound in the branches like that of luck when it turns, or is
luck itself a fixed thing, around which I myself turn or don't,

I remember asking—meaning to ask. Where had I been, for
what felt like forever? Where was I? The tree was itself, and
dying; it resembled, with each scattering of light, all the more

persuasively the kind of argument that can at last let go of them,
all the lovely-enough particulars that, for a time, adorned it:
force is force. The tree was itself. The light fell here and there,

through it. Like history. No—history doesn't fall, we fall through history, the tree is history, I remember thinking, trying not to think it, as I lay exhausted down in its crippled shadow.

Liturgy

for the Mississippi Gulf Coast

To the security guard staring at the Gulf
thinking of bodies washed away from the coast, plugging her ears
against the bells and sirens—sound of alarm—the gaming floor
on the Coast;

To Billy Scarpetta, waiting tables on the Coast, staring at the Gulf
thinking of water rising, thinking of New Orleans, thinking of cleansing
the Coast;

To the woman dreaming of returning to the Coast, thinking of water rising,
her daughter's grave, my mother's grave—underwater—on the Coast;

To Miss Mary, somewhere;

To the displaced, living in trailers along the coast, beside the highway,
in vacant lots and open fields; to everyone who stayed on the Coast,
who came back—or cannot—to the Coast;

To those who died on the Coast.

This is a memory of the Coast: to each his own
recollections, her reclamations, their
restorations, the return of the Coast.

This is a time capsule for the Coast: words of the people
—*don't forget us*—
the sound of wind, waves, the silence of graves,

the muffled voice of history, bull-dozed and buried
under sand poured on the eroding coast,
the concrete slabs of rebuilding the Coast.

This is a love letter to the Gulf Coast, a praise song, a dirge,
invocation and benediction, a requiem for the Gulf Coast.

This cannot rebuild the Coast; it is an indictment, a complaint,
my *logos*—argument and discourse—with the Coast.

This is my *nostos*—my pilgrimage to the Coast, my memory, my
    reckoning—

Native daughter: I am the Gulf Coast.

JEAN TOOMER

Reapers

Black reapers with the sound of steel on stones
Are sharpening scythes. I see them place the hones
In their hip-pockets as a thing that's done,
And start their silent swinging, one by one.
Black horses drive a mower through the weeds,
And there, a field rat, startled, squealing bleeds,
His belly close to ground. I see the blade,
Blood-stained, continue cutting weeds and shade.

Earthquake Blues

Well the cat started actin funny
and the dog howled all night long
I say the cat started actin very frightful
and the birds chirped all night long
The ground began to rumble
As the panic hit the town.

Mr. Earthquake Mr. Earthquake
you don't know good from bad
Mr. Earthquake Mr. Earthquake
you don't know good from bad
You kill the little child in its nursery
You burn up the widow's pad

The buildings started swaying
like a drunk man walking home
The buildings started swaying
like a drunk man walking home
The people they were running
and the hurt folks began to moan

Mr. Earthquake Mr. Earthquake
you don't know good from bad
Mr. Earthquake Mr. Earthquake
you don't know good from bad

You kill the little child in its nursery
You burn up the widow's pad

I got underneath my table
Had my head between my knees
I got underneath the table
Had my head between my knees
The dishes they were rattlin
and the house was rockin me

Mr. Earthquake Mr. Earthquake
you don't know good from bad
Mr. Earthquake Mr. Earthquake
you don't know good from bad
You kill the little child in its nursery
You burn up the widow's pad

I was worried about my baby
Was she safe or was she dead
I was worried about my baby
Was she safe or was she dead
When she phoned and said I'm
ok, Daddy. Then I went on back
to bed.

Mr. Earthquake Mr. Earthquake
you don't know good from bad
Mr. Earthquake Mr. Earthquake
you don't know good from bad
You kill the little child in its nursery
You burn up the widow's pad

Erasure

I can't save the gray wings
molded to sand
like more of the same gritty tapestry.

No merciful dusting of the head
or clearing the belly's burrow
of baby sand crabs.

I believe in the order of things,
what belongs on the beach—smooth shards
of bottle glass, torn jellyfish stinging

in death. Not this fat moth
whose legs struggle out at the sky.
Even I belong to this salt spray,

crush of waves turning
over themselves, surfacing debris.
In the way my feet sink

for the sand's slow erasure.
The moth stays half buried, done in
by the tiny, transparent bodies tunneling

through its middle. The frenzy
if I could hear it
might sound of breaking bones

or see in its eyes—stars begin
as mere beads of determination.
A body will try to right itself.

Someone brave, or foolish
puts the boot down.

Floodsong 2: Water Moccasin's Spiritual

wade in the water
wade in the water, children
wade in the water
god's gon' trouble the water

wade in the water
wade in the water, children
wade in the water
god's gon' trouble the water

wade in
wade in
wade in

        trouble

    in the water
      the water children
    in the water
      trouble the water

god's

        children
   gon'
   in the water
      trouble
   in the water
      trouble
   in the water

                    water
                    water
                    water
god's gon'

Requiem

Oh, I who so wanted to own some earth,
Am consumed by the earth instead:
Blood into river
Bone into land
      The grave restores what finds its bed.

Oh, I who did drink of Spring's fragrant clay,
Give back its wine for other men:
Breath into air
Heart into grass
      My heart bereft—I might rest then.

Ice Storm

Unable to sleep, or pray, I stand
by the window looking out
at moonstruck trees a December storm
has bowed with ice.

Maple and mountain ash bend
under its glassy weight,
their cracked branches falling upon
the frozen snow.

The trees themselves, as in winters past,
will survive their burdening,
broken thrive. And am I less to You,
my God, than they?

Talk of the Animals

A Shepherd's Tale

It's a chilly gray day in late October, and I'm at the Monterey Bay Aquarium standing on the dry side of the glass opposite a school of anchovies. I'm here with my friend Marc, who's in town from New York for a librarians' convention. He's an indexer concerned with taxonomies (schemes of classification) here to find out about the new Internet phenomenon known as folksonomies—taxonomies created by users tagging online content. I hadn't seen Marc in a couple of years, so I drove down from Oakland, where I've been living for the last two months. Marc says the six-foot oval of swirling silver little fish looks like a thumbprint, and he's right. But before they tightened into that oval, when they were only a ribbon of silver waving in the water, they reminded me of the flocks of starlings I would see flying over the field toward the line of trees behind the house where I grew up in Milledgeville, Georgia. Birds and fish have enthralled and transfixed me all my life. I think this has to do in part with the way they move through their environments.

Animals and leaps figured greatly in my childhood. I lay on Nana's thick green carpet in front of her floor-model RCA to watch *Mutual of Omaha's Wild Kingdom*. Silver-haired Marlin Perkins would tell Jim Fowler, twenty-five years his junior, to leap from the jeep or the helicopter onto the back of some fleeing quadruped on the savannah or the snowfield. Johnny Weissmuller as Tarzan ululating and leaping into a river. Frogs and crickets. The young cow that leapt from the truck bed on the Sparta highway. I was riding with my father and his friend to take it to the slaughterhouse. The three little pigs that flinched when the scalpel sliced into their scrotum (but that came later). I remember the occasional fish on the floor that had leapt from one of the aquariums in our house during the night.

By the second grade, I had made many trips to the pet shop in the mall with my father for more tropical fish. At the pet shop, I encountered angelfish, oscars, plecostomus, algae eaters, black mollies, swordtails, guppies, betas, tetras, transparent glassfish, and my favorite, the blind cave fish—eyeless and albino—almost translucent. I'd read the labels on the tanks and try to figure out which fish went with which name before my father told me. The language of the names was almost as entrancing as the fish themselves. Besides the fish, my indulgent parents also allowed me to have a variety of pets: some I picked up in the yard or from down at the creek or from the woods—turtles, frogs, newts, salamanders, fence lizards, dogs, and cats—and some I got from the pet shop—hermit crabs, hamsters, guinea pigs, and a rabbit. And before I discovered the bookstore, my mother would leave me in that same pet shop while she did her shopping. It was there I decided I wanted to be a veterinarian.

Somewhere between the ages of seven and twelve I had outlined a clear plan for becoming a vet. It all came together in my head. But when I turned sixteen, the vet who'd promised me a job back when I was twelve didn't need any help. However, she was able to direct me to a shepherdess who needed a hand. So my first paying job was as a shepherd. I tended a flock of 127 Suffolk sheep. They're the ones with the black faces and legs. In an anthropomorphizing leap of imagination I thought of them as cousins wearing white sweaters. My daily routine entailed feeding the sheep, moving them out to pasture, walking the fence to make sure it didn't need repairing, pitching out the barn and putting down fresh hay, and generally tidying up the barn. There was the weekly run to the feed store, and occasionally the flock needed their hooves trimmed. My already soft hands became softer from the lanolin from handling the sheep.

The following summer a position opened up for me at the vet's clinic. My daily duties at the clinic ranged from taking care of the boarders to assisting the doctor in the operating room to accompanying her on farm calls. While working there I watched a mare foal, assisted in the castrating and spaying of many cats and dogs and the occasional farm animal, and observed a necropsy of a calf. I also held beloved family pets who were beyond help or who'd lived into old age and pain while the doctor injected them with a lethal dose of phenobarbital. I'd grown to know these animals in caring for them, and I could feel the life leave them as they relaxed with a final sigh. Both the doctor and I cried. In ways the people around me had not, the animals I met while working for the vet introduced me to life from birth to death.

I don't know that I decided to become a poet the way I decided to become a veterinarian when I was younger, which felt like a very determined and clear decision. I didn't start writing poetry until late in my freshman year at college, but once I started, it became a way of being and seeing and making sense of the world around me—a way of walking in the world—of moving through my environment. While I do hope to communicate something, I'm not necessarily working toward a message. I feel that writing poems is an exploration. My fascination with animals has resulted in a vocabulary of animal imagery and metaphor that has been bouncing around and growing inside my head since childhood. I think back to a book about the animals of the ocean my mom bought me. She would read it to me at night and show me illustrations of oddly shaped sunfish, looking like swimming pancakes; and the docile whale shark, the world's largest fish; and the fantastic oarfish, looking like a long Japanese dragon; and the luminescent and frightening anglerfish, its mouth overfull of long needle teeth. Learning names and habitats and facts about animals transported me to the far corners of the world and brought me closer to the land where I grew up. Animals shaped me as much as the people around me. I grew up near an older cousin who kept a chicken coop and a chicken yard. She also kept ducks and turkeys. As a matter of fact, several people in the neighborhood kept chickens. I remember hearing crowing roosters holding conversations across the neighborhood when I was growing up. I also remember skeins of Canada geese as well as those huge mesmerizing flocks of starlings streaming and wheeling across the sky. Different types of birds have different wingbeats (I can identify a pileated woodpecker's stuttered flight from a great distance) like different walks or rhythms and measures in music or meters in poetry.

When I was thirteen, three years before becoming a shepherd, I learned about the Swedish scientist Carl Linnaeus in science class. He's considered the father of modern botanical and zoological taxonomy. Linnaeus's system of taxonomy is descriptive; groups and subgroups are formed and narrowed based on physical characteristics shared by group members. In a way, I had experienced this kind of classification within my community—light and dark, red and yellow—and in the greater community with black and white. And *nigger* was in this language of taxonomy as well. This is the taxonomy of the place and time in which I grew up. In Linnaeus's scheme of binomial nomenclature, the ubiquitous mockingbird of my youth is known as *Mimus polyglottos*—the many-tongued mimic. In this case, the scientific language is not only descriptive; it's also wonderfully figurative. The way the mockingbird explores and records his world—sharing that record at any chance—spoke to the poet I would become.

JEAN TOOMER

Beehive

Within this black hive to-night
There swarm a million bees;
Bees passing in and out the moon,
Bees escaping out the moon,
Bees returning through the moon,
Silver bees intently buzzing,
Silver honey dripping from the swarm of bees.
Earth is a waxen cell of the world comb,
And I, a drone, → *human compared to drone*
Lying on my back,
Lipping honey,
Getting drunk with silver honey,
Wish that I might fly out past the moon
And curl forever in some far-off farmyard flower.

— wish to be a flying bee

Black-and-White Dusk at Limantour Beach

With no color but the hue
of fog—the husk of air clustered
in its dewy shroud. To the edges of

the loyal horizon, all was gray and white.

Along the coast I walked, crying. Nothing
could have been brighter beneath life's
glaring veil. With no place breaking open

to reveal the sun's wound. Another
grave of light.

This evening I have no shadow's flight, nothing
dark enough to trail or follow.

Minute by minute nothing
changes. The light only darkening
from the lamp on the other side of absence.

Looking over to the abyss I perceive
a city of women lifting their sleek pelts up through
the Pacific sea.

Their black gaze at me. Their ingots of eyes, boundless
and brooding in wet darkness and salt.

Down we go along the spine of shore. Near the edge,
the crash of dusk overwhelms the spirit.

Their eyes empty me—a gelatinous shell gulling
the echoes of my ghosts. So translucent the wave that lifts

their ghostly bodies to the top of the curve and in a pearled
film of water, their silken tails curve
their heavy bodies into mermaids.

Minute by minute
the seals cluster, black pearls, droplets
bobbing up through the water like blood

from the depth of its slight wound.

Following the body the way blood
follows its wounds.

No place breaking open to brighten
the darkest look of animals.

Sympathy

[handwritten: Sympathize w/ non-human forms → compare to enslaved referenced as mules & work horses but... bird is more elegant → refer to himself w/ elegance]

I know what the caged bird feels, alas!
　　When the sun is bright on the upland slopes;
When the wind stirs soft through the springing grass,
And the river flows like a stream of glass;
　　When the first bird sings and the first bud opes,
And the faint perfume from its chalice steals—
I know what the caged bird feels!

I know why the caged bird beats his wing
　　Till its blood is red on the cruel bars;
For he must fly back to his perch and cling
When he fain would be on the bough a-swing;
　　And a pain still throbs in the old, old scars
And they pulse again with a keener sting—
I know why he beats his wing!　　*[handwritten: lasting]*

I know why the caged bird sings, ah me,
　　When his wing is bruised and his bosom sore,—
When he beats his bars and he would be free;
It is not a carol of joy or glee,
　　But a prayer that he sends from his heart's deep core,
But a plea, that upward to Heaven he flings—
I know why the caged bird sings!

[handwritten: singing for freedom]

The Sea-Turtle and the Shark

Strange but true is the story
of the sea-turtle and the shark—
the instinctive drive of the weak to survive
in the oceanic dark.
Driven,
riven
by hunger
from abyss to shoal,
sometimes the shark swallows
the sea-turtle whole.

Thy sly reptilian marine
withdraws,
into the shell
of his undersea craft,
his leathery head and the rapacious claws
that can rip
a rhinoceros' hide
or strip
a crocodile to fare-thee-well;
now,
inside the shark,
the sea-turtle begins the churning seesaws
of his descent into pelagic hell;
then . . . *then,*
with ravenous jaws
that can cut sheet steel scrap,
the sea-turtle gnaws
. . . and gnaws . . . and gnaws . . .

his way in a way that appalls—
his way to freedom,
beyond the vomiting dark,
beyond the stomach walls
of the shark.

snark as masters?
want to transcend
- freedom beyond
labor & enslavement
--think society & social
constructs made
by man

RICHARD WRIGHT

#175

      Coming from the woods,
A bull has a lilac sprig
      Dangling from a horn.

HARRYETTE MULLEN

European Folk Tale Variant

for the archives of Toni Cade Bambara

The way the story goes, a trespassing towheaded pre-teen barged into the rustic country cottage of a nuclear family of anthropomorphic bruins. [*human-like qualities*] Her motivation? Who can be sure? Some say the youthful offender was an innocent maiden who lost her sense of direction in the lush growth of the virgin pine forest. Or perhaps the elders of her tribe had neglected to attend to her proper socialization. In any case, this flaxen-haired vixen perpetrated a "B and E," a felony punishable by law. The incorrigible pre-adolescent didn't stop with trespassing, or even with breaking and entering. The finicky home invader helped herself to generous portions of the ursine honey eaters' whole grain breakfast cereal, vandalized their heirloom antique furniture. Then, after tiring herself out with so much wanton destruction, the platinum blonde delinquent took a refreshing beauty nap in the bruin family's bedroom—just like she thought she was a guest at a cozy bed and breakfast inn. Returning from their fishing expedition, the family could barely express their shock and dismay, seeing the shambles the puerile hoodlum had made of their woodland homestead. Despite their emotional trauma, they successfully expelled the rude intruder from their charming bungalow. With the assistance of the neighborhood crime [*over policing*] patrol, law enforcement officers were able to apprehend and incarcerate the callow miscreant, who has been sentenced to juvenile detention. Attorneys representing the Ursidae family interests have filed suit against the criminally negligent parents of the wayward youth, and expect that the bruins will be awarded a substantial sum for emotional distress as well as for extensive damage to their property.

expect ....

WENDY S. WALTERS

Man Raised as Chicken

Locked in a chicken coop for years, a young boy acquired
the habits of birds. When he escaped no one knew how
to treat him. Doctors tied him to a hospital bed until
they could decide what to do. For twenty years he conspired
change the weather. Questions of narrative reliability arise—
Who would do that to a child? What's the temperature now?
How did he go to the bathroom? Can we get back to normal?
Do not think this is real, for nothing is left to inspire
hope if we treat each other like food. To test goodwill,
Let's amplify the life. Locked in a chicken coop to revise
family, a young boy acquired affection for the brood. Formal
lyrical protocol keeps me from singing why I think
this is. But if a boy can feel with the heart of a bird, I surmise
I know little of men or what it means to be mistaken for one.

Far

Inland suffers its foxes: full-moon fox, far-flung fox—flung him yonder!
went the story—or some fox worn like a weasel round the neck. Foxes
are a simple fact, widespread and local and observable— *Vulpes fulva,* the
common predator, varying in actual color from red to black to rust to tawny
brown, pale only in the headlights.

It's that this far inland the appearance of a fox is more reference than
metaphor. Or the appearance is a demonstration. Sudden appearance, big
like an impulse; or the watcher gains a gradual awareness—in the field,
taking shape and, finally, familiar. The line of sight's fairly clear leaving
imagination little to supply. It's a fact to remember, though, seeing the
fox and where or, at night, hearing foxes (and where). The fox appearing,
coming into view, as if to meet the speaker.

Push comes to shove. Mistah Fox arriving avec luggage, sans luggage.

The Spider Speaks

No choice but to spin,
the life given.

Mother warned me
I would wake one dawn

to a sun no longer yellow,
to an expanse of blue,

no proper word
to name it. Weaving

the patterned threads
of my life, each day

another web and the next.
If instead I could carve

my message in stone,
would it mean more?

I have only this form
to give. When the last

silvery strand leaves
my belly, I will see

what colour the sun
has become.

The Hummingbird

Bright whirligig that knows no grief,
sudden gem whose engine
is diligent and beatific,
in pure communion,
I've opened and taken you
deep into my being.

Scion to your quick colors,
your tiny hosannas, I poise
before my love's body
become a thousand thimbles of weeping
for dawn,
keen galaxy I'd test and savor
with a deft, regaling bill:
all this majesty is for me—

Now the hours are deities
of nectar and sweat.
Now the hours are flower-gorged,
filled with his breath—

Suddenly, I'm flying
backward,
fleet hovering in the moment,
breakneck marionette:
grit gone, God yes,
and panic's balcony:
the carnage in the eye burned away.

The Herd

Some of the light, some of the first light
arrived so softly it could have been dew
drawn from the night air, and in the creamy-
blue distance thunderheads flickered.

They were still sleeping then, scattered
under trees or in groups in the open,
their slate-colored flanks lightening.

Overnight three had been killed, but the wild dogs
were gone now and the scavengers too,
and the lake began to show dawn its muddy edges.

What was surprising was that they ever slept
at all—with so many things alive in the dark,
but they slept well, dreaming exactly what they
dreamed they should dream, and when the strongest one
rolled back the silence with a long, throbbing yawn,

the others answered, divvying up the air
with staccato croaks, shrill bleats and near-
growls—some with front legs still bent
under them, some with eyes caught shining
as if they had never before seen the world.

No one knew how long they had been here
or what to call them. Or how it was that they came
to understand themselves, what to do, where to go.

But they moved together like slow wind,
as a wind moves from one place to another,
dying off but rising again, the same wind moving.

And when the must broke into their blood
they coupled fiercely, almost in panic, as if
one by one they were beginning to drown—the heat
sliding over each in turn like the shadow of a cloud.

.   .   .

Once it had cleared the treetops, the sun paved
the veldt bright yellow, and the stilt-legged birds
that had been chitter-whistling since early early,
quieted; some stood in the shallows
stabbing the lake for lazy, flat-headed fish.

The herd was eating too, nudging each other for room,
nostrils flexing wet and open. You might have
thought they'd been made for nothing but
filling their mouths, so content did they seem,
tugging at the stringy greens with their square teeth.

They were not stupid; though sometimes when weather
changed unexpectedly, they would simply stampede
barrel-eyed while the rain snapped against their backs.
And if one among them bore some odd marking,
when it reached a certain age, the others
drove it away with head-butts and hard kicks.

I saw it happen once: a female with a bronze-colored face
instead of the usual gray, limped a short ways
behind the herd, her right foreleg fractured.
Each time she tried to rejoin they attacked—mainly
the bulls and ranking cows—stomping, frothing,
fussing up immense heaves of dust.

The wounded animal seemed confused, not seeing, not
being able to see what was wrong, unable to keep
from following, just as the attackers couldn't
stop themselves, couldn't understand what stranged
inside their skulls to turn them against their own.

. . .

The dogs were made for this—
their sharp, felt-furred ears barely visible,
gliding above the high weeds by the lake,
and when they took the open field their feet
kissed the earth for allowing such speed
and the taste of meat and they were upon her
and the air turned over, so heavy with the smell
of blood, it was nearly animal itself.

Hard to say what went on inside the herd
with death blossoming right there,
or if any had actually watched the kill,
or if it made a difference either way.
The dogs would always be there
blind but for their teeth, and the herd
would continue to find the sunrise
next to the dark, returning from sleep
to offer their young to the flat world.

And was it anything like sorrow
that brought them back days later
to scuff the ground where that one
with the new face had fallen?

Or just some dumb itch
of memory, some lizard's blink
of déjà-vu: the future circling
to take them along.

CORNELIUS EADY

Speed

I have seen the swallows spin
Above the bell tower,

Quick feathers gathering air.
If an arrow could think

These are the handsome moves
It would choose for itself.

In Florence, the swallow
Is a swirl of pigment,

A blurred hunger under
Dappled light.

I am big and chunky,
I am dressed incorrectly,

And I have yet to think
At the speed of the world.

ISHMAEL REED

Points of View

The pioneers and the indians
disagree about a lot of things
for example, the pioneer says that
when you meet a bear in the woods
you should yell at him and if that
doesn't work, you should fell him
The indians say that you should
whisper to him softly and call him by
loving nicknames
No one's bothered to ask the bear
what he thinks

Excerpted from the book *Ishmael Reed: New and Collected Poems,*
1964–2006. © 1988 by Ishmael Reed. Permission granted by
Lowenstein-Yost Associates, Inc.

WANDA COLEMAN

Requiem for a Nest

the winged thang built her dream palace
amid the fine green eyes of a sheltering bough
she did not know it was urban turf
disguised as serenely delusionally rural
nor did she know the neighborhood was rife
with slant-mawed felines and those long-taloned
swoopers of prey. she was ignorant of the acidity & oil
that slowly polluted the earth, and was never
to detect the serpent coiled one strong limb below

following her nature she flitted and dove
for whatever blades twigs and mud
could be found under the humming blue
and created a hatchery for her spawn
not knowing all were doomed

CLARENCE MAJOR

Surfaces and Masks

XXX

They cut down the last tree
        on the *campo*
                where I sit
near the old boatyard at San Trovaso.
        The birds also miss it:
                they fly into the space
where it once stood and
                        sink,
        as though in quicksand.
I can now see the path,
                church
        and castle.
But did I need to?
Rain now
        falls hard to the ground,
with no leaves or limbs
                to pause on.
Yet, when did Venice
        seriously
      need trees or gardens
              not secretly
kept behind stone walls?

TOI DERRICOTTE

The Minks

In the backyard of our house on Norwood,
there were five hundred steel cages lined up,
each with a wooden box
roofed with tar paper;
inside, two stories, with straw
for a bed. Sometimes the minks would pace
back and forth wildly, looking for a way out;
or else they'd hide in their wooden houses, even when
we'd put the offerings of raw horse meat on their trays, as if
they knew they were beautiful
and wanted to deprive us.
In spring the placid kits
drank with glazed eyes.
Sometimes the mothers would go mad
and snap their necks.
My uncle would lift the roof like a god
who might lift our roof, look down on us
and take us out to safety.
Sometimes one would escape.
He would go down on his hands and knees,
aiming a flashlight like
a bullet of light, hoping to catch
the orange gold of its eyes.
He wore huge boots, gloves
so thick their little teeth couldn't bite through.
"They're wild," he'd say. "Never trust them.
Each afternoon when I put the scoop of raw meat rich
with eggs and vitamins on their trays,
I'd call to each a greeting.
Their small thin faces would follow as if slightly curious.

In fall they went out in a van, returning
sorted, matched, their skins hanging down on huge metal
hangers, pinned by their mouths.
My uncle would take them out when company came
and drape them over his arm—the sweetest cargo.
He'd blow down the pelts softly
and the hairs would part for his breath
and show the shining underlife which, like
the shining of the soul, gives us each
character and beauty.

Possum

1
A child points
                outside,
beside a rusted cypress:
this scuttling.

They squat together, child and woman
peering into the darkness, under
a rind of light, seeing

a screwed face and bad dentistry,
a jagged pelt aglow, its dirty tallow
burning just outside their window.

It snarls at them,

at these two shadows peering, one
delighted by fear, and one
amazed.

Is this how the past approaches?

2
I see them,
growling and raising their long
claws

in the razored light,
these dogs.

But I don't do what they suppose, fall
down, faint, overcome by possibility,
by fear, by habit,

or pretend that tooth, claw, and an imperfect
sense of mystery are the only defenses.

No, I turn my nose to them,
show them my teeth, fierce snarling
to let them know: I am a poet!

3
Fifteen baby possums will fit in the bowl
of a teaspoon.

4
From the compost
         rinds and rottings,

from the garbage
         peels,

from the shadows' darkness, darkness,
         this guttered meal and all its redolence.

What we were, what we were shaped to be,
fasts on waste.

What we are points its vulpine head and sniffs
but the next minute has no scent, and the minute
before is already carrion: eat.

In memory's midden this rubbish eater:
sucker of yolk and entrails, the biter of mice
coveting the blueing breads, bones, and maggotted meat.
Our appetites are no bigger than we are.

From the compost
	rinds and rottings,

from the garbage
	peels,

from the shadows' darkness, darkness,
	this guttered meal and all its redolence.

Why do you dine on refuse and avoid the banquet?

5
Possums are immune to rattlesnake venom.

6
And the possum has mastered these lessons:

of persimmons—
time and energy vibrating on a string of light
equals sweetness;

of night—
in the absence of color all things reveal
themselves by shape, smell, or trembling;

of prehensile tails—
look down! The world is uncertain.

We shake like Quakers above a molten fire,
small embers spinning on a ball of fire;
swaying back and forth, on our prehensile tails,
signal lights before an impossible engine;

of playing possum—
this is faith: arise and walk!

of jacklighting—
stunned we hold ourselves still
on a dark branch, death?

Or a lover's touch just there—ah! Still.

7
Infant possums inside their mother's pouch,
inhaling the same air, suffocate.

8
The hounds bay
and Webster's voice bawls
through the piney woods. Trembling,
the kudzu turns green ears
to the distance: listen.

The mind runs, climbs,
scuttles, leaps, scramble-stumbles
and burrows into briared dream.

Hiding for one brief moment before
the rending, the night's belly torn
open, its blasted heart pounding
ca choom, ca choom, ca choom, blood spilling
its red sand, its red sand, its red sand, spilling

for one brief moment.

Fireflies blink under a stand of pine,
an owl calls *hu hu, hu-huuuuu,*
hu hu, hu-huuuuu.

On its dark branch, the jacklighted
moon glints at a stunned world,

and a possum scurries away.

9
In Vernon,
a colored child is given a possum patty
for breakfast, a patty sweet with salt
and red-peppered. She holds greasy fingers
up to her grandmother. *Meat, Big Mama,
meat!* and is given another.

In Vernon, a colored child is given
a possum patty from a heat-smoky skillet,
and it is salt-sweet, greasy, and generously
peppered, large enough to fill both her hands.

The Appaloosa

The one horse you gave me
you took back when she went insane,
when she began to chew wood
instead of the expensive grain
we bought from the feed store,
the grain that had the sweet smell
of molasses and was good for even
us to chew. She turned into
an ugly thing with her wild thoughts,
and I forgot about the beauty
expected of her when her blanket
filled out and complemented
her chestnut body and the name
the Nez Percé gave her. She rotted
and began to stink of promises
gone wrong, of gods avenging
their defilement. A man who knew
what to do with useless horses
came and took her away in
a wooden trailer she tried to chew,
and my tears welled up in huge drops
before they splattered on the ground,
as I trembled and realized I would have
to give up her own ghost for her,
ghost which she did not have, ghost
which she came here beautifully without.

April Lyric / All I Know Is

The sound of water running down the leg of the man on the bus
    three seats away
is softer than I would have imagined, if I had ever imagined this scene:
Some man pissing quietly as he sat, ashamed, cross-legged, hoping the bus
would reach his stop before anyone noticed the stain streaking the tan
    corduroy pants
he wore, before anyone noticed the drops falling from his sodden cuff,
    before noses
twitched reflexively and tracked the scent straight to this spot.
Before he got caught, the man may have worried someone would call out,
Shit! and demand the driver stop and deal with this indecency that
    wasn't really
an indecency, but an accident, matter of timing, for all we know.

It's so easy for me to think up reasons: a bladder shriveled from some
    medicine
his doctor prescribed; or the cup of coffee gulped to pull through the last
    hour of a shift;
or an afternoon filled with pints of beer; or, maybe, I'm guessing,
    nightmares of childhood.

There are obligations beyond the social. There are obligations beyond
    the polite
demands the mind makes. I think of Bob, blind and devoted to the tactile.
    Touch
and touch and more touch, gets him through his day. I've seen the little
    game of tug he plays
with the neighbor's dog, making the dog pull the biscuits from his mouth,
    sharing a kiss

with the mulatto shepherd, a quick brush of lips and tongue—sometimes
  more. Sometimes, more.
A deep exploration of the other's mouth, searching, sweeping the roof and
  floor for crumbs.
He doesn't give reasons when he leaves, or when he stays, as he sometimes
  does, petting
the dog, scratching the itch, rubbing its belly the way it likes while it moans,
  thumps its leg.
If he could see the smile on the dog's face, the broad canine grin of
  sexual pleasure,
he might stop, or he might not. I don't know. I don't know what he would
  do. I don't know.

What the Land Remembers

April in Eatonton

Eliot called it "the cruelest month," but it truly is the best time to go there. To Eatonton when the temperature is reasonable, not brutal as it is in the middle of the summer, say July or August, when the heat and the humidity make you sure you've committed a grave sin and God is punishing you for it.

Eatonton, right around Easter when serious gardeners lower their plants into their individual patches of earth. Anyone who's read her almanac knows she ought to plant at that moment. And why not? Look around. If God has cultivated the rest of the world and a new rain has brought forth the frailness of fruit or flower, then we should follow God and start our own planting. Not because of so-called true religion, but because of common sense.

April in Eatonton is a holy time. I am sure of it, sinner though I may be.

Suddenly, the pines and pecans seem taller. They've been that way from the very beginning, but as I drive, I haven't noticed until the sky turns blue and demands that I bear witness. Then I do bear witness. I look through the glass of my windshield and into the horizon that in its benevolence mutes its brightness and there they are: the trees.

The trees in April almost don't remind me of the earlier, uglier purpose. What the branches were used for, hanging and such. How can I dwell on anyone's terror, even my own, at the sight of those trees? The pointed leaves of the pecans, the dear spikes of the pine needles?

The peaches haven't arrived yet, but my mind will move to a few months later. Inevitably. Big, fat, juicy peaches in their smutty glory. Those peaches seem innocent in the imagination, though once I think on it, I recall that they remind me of a first kiss—awkward, but then wait a minute. Here comes the flick of the wet, delicious tongue. A sin. Yes, Lord, a good and nasty sin. I wipe my mouth, but before I do that, I smack my lips a few times.

What else would be left after having witnessed joy beyond compare? Nothing. Once I drive along Highway 441, past Madison and the road through the trees (before I get to Beaver Dam), it might be a good time to close my eyes forever. I deserve a really satisfying death, quick and without pain. And a good home going, too, with an expensive casket, lots of grievers, and a preacher expounding ad nauseam on my life: my selfless deeds, my fine looks, my boundless love for others. The *agape* kind of love, I mean, not my indecent exploits. This wouldn't be one of those other scandalous, southern funerals you have heard so much about.

. . .

Before, the land was just that, and April was even better then. This place was cleaner before the car dealerships, barbecue shacks, Walmarts and those awful new developments up and down the highway.

Even further back: two hundred years ago. When there were the Creek and the Cherokee. A couple of hundred years ago, there wasn't any cotton. It was mostly Indians, whom they call Native Americans now, but they weren't that either because it wasn't *America* yet. Or even *Georgia*.

Creek and Cherokee. Those names, only in their own language. And if they didn't always live in peace with each other, there were no major wars. Those skirmishes between tribes might have seemed so at first, but when the real killing began, when the others arrived and took the land and then changed the laws for the removal—for the cotton that needed to be grown—when the killings after that started up, and *The Journey Where They Cried*, the skirmishes couldn't compare.

. . .

It was 1794 when Eli Whitney found a way to separate the good from the bad. More specifically, the seeds from the bolls. Before, it was one pound of cotton a day. After, it was fifty. They started loading up the ships even more across that water. They started tight-packing those teenagers from Africa.

It doesn't matter if he stole the invention from a slave, or from his benefactress, Catherine Greene, or if he came up with the gin on his own. Think of him, a guest in her home. Tinkering with his little, rude inventions. A man stewing in the juice of mediocrity, thinking about his life and all he hadn't done. He was afraid. He felt failure and the blankness of his legacy breathing down his neck. And when night fell, and he was in bed, perhaps he was listening to the creaking of Mrs. Greene's step over the heart pine floors, imagining if she dared to detour and open his door an hour after midnight. This was, after all, her home. Maybe he hoped she would stand in the doorway, her long braid over her left shoulder.

That was the night. In the day, perhaps she—*Catherine*, if they were lovers, *Mistress Greene* if not—came into the parlor and leaned over him as he stood at a table and pondered his bits of metal and drawings. The smell of her—*perfume* if they weren't lovers, *scent* if they were—brought about an epiphany. He found the truth and the light right here in Georgia, in the house of a lady. He found out how to take those seeds out of short staple cotton and make that money multiply.

Or maybe, a slave found out how to do it. Or *servant*, as a slave was more politely called. And so the scent that hovered over Eli Whitney and brought forth the muse of the machine was not that of a gentle lady, but the funk and sweat and hopelessness of a dark man.

That cotton gin turned into a prophecy of its own: what the land would become, what the people and the folk turned into. It wasn't for some grand concept that they removed the Indians and it changed from a name no one calls out anymore. The land changed for one thing only: cotton.

.   .   .

This land is called *Eatonton* now, the little town I'm driving through, but actually, I'm calling it *home*.

And I certainly can't agree with Eliot that this month is cruel. The man's got it wrong. Nothing's cruel in Eatonton in April. Because—*because*—look at the land. At least, look at what remains, not what's been taken.

ROBERT HAYDEN

Locus

for Ralph

Here redbuds like momentary trees
        of an illusionist;
here Cherokee rose, acacia, and mimosa;
here magnolias—totemic flowers
        wreathing legends of this place.
Here violent metamorphosis,
        with every blossom turning
deadly and memorial soldiers,
their sabres drawn, charging
        firewood shacks,
apartheid streets. Here wound-red earth
        and blinding cottonfields,
rock hills where sachems counseled,
where scouts gazed stealthily
        upon the glittering death march
of De Soto through Indian wilderness.
        Here mockingbird and
cottonmouth, fury of rivers.
Here swamp and trace and bayou
        where the runagate hid,
the devil with Spanish pistols rode.
        Here spareness, rankness, harsh
brilliances; beauty of what's hardbitten,
knotted, stinted, flourishing
        in despite, on thorny meagerness
thriving, twisting into grace.
        Here symbol houses

where the brutal dream lives out its lengthy
dying. Here the past, adored and
            unforgiven. Here the past—
soulscape, Old Testament battleground
of warring shards whose weapons kill.

Jaguaripe

Everything begins with a hill where
a church   bar is built   a city founded.
Our legs thicken to those of mules

as we carry clay to the top. The roads
rolling down slope into town   cobblestones
where dirt peaks until the next rain.

The pain of place is without end   backs
mighty as earth. All of this so a girl can sit
on her porch   a red ribbon in her hair matching

her Sunday skirt. She stares at hibiscus yet
smells caramel as bees leave one blossom for another.
Whose love is this?

At the port   barnacles attach
themselves to the banks. Those eyes see
what they want. Crabs the color of fire

walk in packs as gulls hover   these will not
be eaten   the blue ones will. A boy throws
a bucket with a chicken carcass inside.

There is a rope tied to the handle already
knotted to the pole where the boy waits. Beneath
cobalt water shrimp are clawed   torn

slowly   death visible in transparent bodies.
Greedy blue crabs fight over fowl bones
as the boy pulls the bucket to the deck.

He holds one crab between thumb   index
finger   top of the head to abdomen   no
cuts   no blood scented air. Clouds of sugar   burnt

rose petal waves break at the foot of a white house.
That prison of salt where captives were locked   flooded.
They drowned   a wretched eighteenth century.

Oh the apparitions above this water. Those believers
in one dark woman's quiet   decent power see everything.
Those with disbelief have taken to the forest

as palm colored lizards   blue macaws   spider
monkeys. Restless sleep or no sleep at all
as a boy strokes a wall of that once water logged place.

He touches his chest. Insides rumble so much so
he must rest near a gate infested with moss. He sees
girls frolicking in a banana grove. Later men

sing   play instruments in the general store.
An audience gathers   perhaps this Sunday
is joy   silver over a watery crypt.

What There Was

Pine, catalpa, pin oak, persimmon,
but not tree.

Hummingbird, hoot owl, martin, crow,
but not bird.

Cannas, honeysuckle, cockscomb, rose,
but not flower.

Wood smoke, corn, dust, outhouse,
but not stench.

A spider spinning in a rain barrel,
the silver dipper by the back porch,
tadpoles shimmying against a concrete bank,
but not silence.

A cotton row, a bucket lowered into a well,
a red dirt road, a winging crow,
but not distance.

A rooster crowing, cows lowing in the evening,
wasps humming beneath the eaves, hounds
baying, hot grease, but not music.

My mother running away at fifteen,
my grandmother lifting a truck to save a life,
an uncle at Pearl Harbor, Webster sitting
at the back of the bus when he looked as white
as they did, but not stories.

The entrails of a slaughtered sow, the child born
with a goat's face, the cousin laid on a railroad
track, the fire that burned it all, but not death.

This poem, a snuff tin sated with the hair
of all our dead, my mother's nighttime talks
with her dead father, my great-grandmother's
clothes passed down, passed down, but not memory.

Wind Talker

> *Ocian in view! O! the joy.*
> —William Clark

If I could make my words
dress they naked selves in blackberry juice
lay down on a piece a bark, sheep
or onion skin, like Massa do

If I could send a letter home to my wife
float it in the wind, on wings or water

I'd tell her 'bout Katonka
an all the wide an high places
this side a the big river.
How his family, numbering three
for every star in the sky
look like a forest when they graze together
turn into the muddy M'soura
when they thunder along, faster than any horse
making the grass lay down
long after the quiet has returned.
How they don't so much as raise a tail
when I come 'round with my wooly head
an tobacco skin, like I'm one a them
making the Arikara an Mandan think me
"Big Medicine"
Katonka, who walks like man.

Today, we stood on the edge a all this
looked out at so much water
the mountains we crossed to get here
seem a little smaller.

As I watch fish the size a cabins dance in the air
and splash back in the water like children playing
I think 'bout her an if we gone ever be free
then I close my eyes an pray
that I don't live long enough
to see Massa make this ugly too.

LUCILLE CLIFTON

mulberry fields

they thought the field was wasting
and so they gathered the marker rocks and stones and
piled them into a barn   they say that the rocks were shaped
some of them scratched with triangles and other forms   they
must have been trying to invent some new language they say
the rocks went to build that wall there guarding the manor and
some few were used for the state house   *fenced land*
crops refused to grow
i say the stones marked an old tongue and it was called eternity
and pointed toward the river   i say that after that collection
no pillow in the big house dreamed   i say that somewhere under
here moulders one called alice whose great grandson is old now
too and refuses to talk about slavery   i say that at the
masters table only one plate is set for supper   i say no seed
can flourish on this ground once planted then forsaken   wild
berries warm a field of bones
bloom how you must i say   *time*

moving forward?

260

I Am Black and the Trees Are Green

so you point
and say the woods are beautiful
like men standing on shores
of Africa enjoying the sun on their skin
the white sand touching the water blue
the new slaves as invisible as conversation

supressed
white & blue

The Maple Remains

Vicksburg, Mississippi, May 16, 1919

For the general good
Such, even the smell
Is customary; like figs
Gray and gamy, rotting
Among the orchard mulch.

And an old woman
Remembers her children
As little monkeys for its branches,
Their hinged arms and legs are
Indistinguishable at dusk.

She remembers the clearing
When she and her husband
First arrived in Vicksburg;
How Charles leaned against
The trunk, his face washed
With shadow and smoke;

How he looked at the land
The crest and its antiseptic
Slopes and said, "This is home."

The old woman remembers
And pleads for its felling
And a young man gazing
Among the throngs responds:

"What was done here
Last night, was done
For you and for every
Woman and for every
Girl in Warren County."

Tallahatchie Lullabye, Baby

Emmett Till (1941–1955)

cattail cast tattles Till tale,
lowing low along the hollow;
cricket chirrup and ribbit lick-up.
what's chucked the 'hatchie swallow.

skin scow skiffing upon pond scum skin,
going slow along the hollow.
now may mayfly alight brown brow.
what's chucked the 'hatchie swallow.

maybe bye baby bye baby by and by,
lowing low along the hollow.
we will slip the knot not slip will we?
what's chucked the 'hatchie swallow.

who's a bruise to whose hue, 'hatchie?
going slow along the hollow?
whose a bruise to bruise hue, 'hatchie?
what's chucked the 'hatchie swallow.

Kodak flash tattles Till tale
going slow among the hollow.
who's a bruise to bruise hue?
swallow what the 'hatchie chucks.

JUNE JORDAN

Out in the Country of My Country

Peterborough, New Hampshire

Filling my eyes with flowers of no name
that I can call aloud: This northernmost retreat
of white pine or aching birch
of meadow mouth opening the body of a perfect land
that throws away birdsong on the rushes
of hard rain

Testing my heart with precipice and crest
accumulating timber trails or fern
beside the mica sparkling road that peaks
at mountain heights of granite situated
next to purple lilac feeling out the light
of short cold days

Choosing my mind between mosquitoes and the moon
that dominates a darkness larger than the stars
close by: I (what do you suppose)
I battle with the spirits of a winterkill
that spoils the summer berries: Blunts the nipple points
of love

Chasing my face among displacements of a stream
I behold the Indian: I become the slave
again I am hunting / I am hunted in these snowy woods
again I am eagle / I am scrambling on the summit rocks
I slip I scream I soar I seek the dancing of the spirits
from the grave

Three Days of Forest, a River, Free

The dogs have nothing better
to do than bark; duty's whistle
slings a bright cord
around their throats.
I'll stand here all night
if need be, no more real
than a tree when no moon shines.

The terror of waking is a trust
drawn out unbearably
until nothing, not even love,
makes it easier, and yet
I love this life:

three days of forest,
the mute riot of leaves.

Who can point out a smell
but a dog? The way is free
to the river. Tell me,
Lord, how it feels
to burst out like a rose.

Blood rises in my head—
I'm there.
Faint tongue, dry fear,
I think I lost you to the dogs,
so far off now they're no
more than a chain of bells
ringing darkly, underground.

American Light

Cardinals land
on a branch, female and male.
The sky shivers
in puddles created of night rain.
Speckled particles dance
in a path of light, so it seems
it doesn't matter what's in the road.
Then the shadow of a black oak
leans forward like a wounded man.

The lit landscape conceives
a shadow, its face dark, wide-open,
its eyes bloodshot
from what had come before.

.   .   .

In the lit landscape, in its peeled
back places, making the space
uncomfortable, representing no fault
in the self is a shadow
of a gesture of wanting, coveting
the American light.

constructed

A shadow on ships, in fields
for years, for centuries even, in heat
colored by strokes of red, against
the blue-white light—and in it
I realize I recognize myself.

.   .   .

And still the light
fills wind-tossed branches,
makes clouds iridescent
islands in the sky. And still
the same light (for nothing
in nature is private)
insists on a shadow in the road.

   •   •   •

I step into my shadow
as if not to take it anymore,
and wonder where I am going.

Sweet sad shadow, sun charred
on the open road, I don't want
any trouble, don't wish
to be troubled, but when the sun
goes down on this aged,
dirt road, will I end
in the dark woods, or make it home?

Look Ahead, Look South: the future

Looking at my bad attitude toward the pastoral

& only seeing myself on one of those red dirt roads
I'd seen from the air, caught unlucky

w/night more palpable every minute, that
for future

Southern Song

I want my body bathed again by southern suns, my soul
    reclaimed again from southern land. I want to rest
    again in southern fields, in grass and hay and clover
    bloom; to lay my hand again upon the clay baked by a
    southern sun, to touch the rain-soaked earth and smell
    the smell of soil.

I want to rest unbroken in the fields of southern earth;
    freedom to watch the corn wave silver in the sun and
    mark the splashing of a brook, a pond with ducks and
    frogs and count the clouds.

I want no mobs to wrench me from my southern rest; no
    forms to take me in the night and burn my shack and
    make for me a nightmare full of oil and flame.

I want my careless song to strike no minor key; no fiend to
    stand between my body's southern song—the fusion of
    the South, my body's song and me.

ED ROBERSON

Wave

everyone sees the sea coming down the beach
everyone calls it the white horses.
nobody's language is ever mistaken
they never fail to come called
on any shore they are broken to.
there is a man who has seen the distance
in the desert do just that
same break   at a walk.
he calls the horizon the white horses
and i have called my sight the reef.

i can imagine that black men call them
the white dogs
and that for the same reasons
the earth could come to call the spray
stars of the milky way
the middle passage
coming down the black sand space
like it was as due as justice
a simple wave   landing and
towing the blanched shell it has taken back like slaves.

EVIE SHOCKLEY

her table mountain

every poet has a table mountain tucked right beneath epidermis, waiting for the prick of evening wind for release.
—p. g.

they'd been to the same city, but you wouldn't have known it. he came
   home
blissing about jacaranda in bloom; on her visit, winter hid

color behind the thick gray of clouds and rain, except for those pastel
houses hiking up the steep slopes of the bo-kaap, a little squint-and-

see-san-francisco quarter early muslims had raised like a garden
in the town. he sang in liquid tones of how the atlantic reached down

and crooked her blue finger round this lucky cape before giving the sea
bed over to the indian ocean. she recognized that body,

too, instinctively: there, the same wet cradle and grave it was where she
knew it best—but there it was also jailer and jail, cruel cup in which

rose the knuckle of land where mandela and sisulu couched their hopes
across an ignorant count of years. his table mountain was a vast,

gentle lover. *i spent the clearest night of my life on its summit.*
all the universe was caught up in my throat. she recalled her ascent.

the cable car, as it lugged itself from high to heights, twirled her once
around in a slow, careful dance across the sky. even gray, the views

were punctured with beauty: the steel blue bars of ocean rolling into
the waterfront; buildings pushed unpredictably into parallels

or angles with each other—like a jar of pearly rectangular
buttons spilled, splayed, and then swept into a haphazard constellation—

arrayed from water to mountain base and out onto the flats in an
endless shimmering; the craggy stone of the mountain face foreboding

an unforgiving terrain. she spent the coldest afternoon of her
life on that summit, coatless in thirty-degree winds, her numb fingers

cramped around her camera, ankles turning on the trail's uneven
rock. between billows of mist, she gazed down into a city that tried

to cut out its own heart—it still bore the grassy scar where district six
had thrummed—and she loved it: utterly, open-eyed, as fiercely as if

it were hers or herself, despite the miserable august weather,
despite the acid tang she detected in his *place of sweet waters*,

despite the history of peoples chained and chaining, killed and killing,
that hung over it like the clouds over that prehistoric mountain.

from "Juneteenth: The Bicentennial Poem"

1. The Dream Realized

> *the waters don't sing in that land*
> *they run sly and silent deep in the ground*

north county
for inez talamantez

The freeway is a river
of light rounding the base of
Mt. Soledad, its distant
drone a part of the night. I've
watched in the darkness as the
river dimmed to the fitful
passing of solitary
cars and heard the coyotes
in the canyon crying their
survival to the strange land

I booted up one day, walked
out across the mesa that
fronts along my place till the
land was a shallow cup around
me and the houses were lost
in the distance on its
rim. The plants were the only
life I saw—muted greens dry
browns bursts of loud purple and
lighter blues, brilliant in the
spring light; something rustled the

undergrowth; a jet murmured
in the softly clabbered sky.

The Indian dead are here
buried beneath Spanish place
names and the cities of the
pioneers and the droning
silence is witness to what
each has claimed, what each owned.
My father's grave is here some
where his tale lost like that jet
in clabber his children
scattered along the river
voices singing to the night.

Tap-Root

i
Concrete and steel drew the M'ssippi
back like a fist. Scythe blade swung
through dry harvests. Plows turned
soil hard enough to raise the Blues.

Muddy Waters sprang whole, dry-
heaved from the knotted center
of a plank-wood shack.
Shook hisself loose of blood,
dirt, moonshine, the ass-dark end
of a mule and was gone.

ii
Since, twisters have spun the shack
'round, bent its insides out, till it
vomited its secrets on boot-dust roads.
Now tourists use splintered slivers
of history as toothpicks.

A little ways down the road
you can squander a week's pay,
sleep in an old slave shack.
Spend a day picking cotton.
Smile for pictures.

iii
The M'ssippi used to cover
these parts, until they dammed

it up, held its tongue like words
you choke back in church
to keep your insides from escaping.

Staring across dusty fields
you can ache the need for river.
Almost drown in longing for waters
that won't come here no more.

MARILYN NELSON

Last Talk with Jim Hardwick

A "found" poem

When I die I will live again.
By nature I am a conserver.
I have found Nature
to be a conserver, too.
Nothing is wasted
or permanently lost
in Nature. Things
change their form,
but they do not cease
to exist. After
I leave this world
I do not believe I am through.
God would be a bigger fool
than even a man
if He did not conserve
the human soul,
which seems to be
the most important thing
He has yet done in the universe.
When you get your grip
on the last rung of the ladder
and look over the wall
as I am now doing,
you don't need their proofs:
You see.
You know
you will not die.

History as Apple Tree

Cocumscussoc is my village,
the western arm of Narragansett
Bay; Canonicus chief sachem;
black men escape into his tribe.

How does patent not breed heresy?
Williams came to my chief
for his tract of land,
hunted by mad Puritans,
founded Providence Plantation;
Seekonk where he lost
first harvest, building, plant,
then the bay from these natives:
he set up trade.
With Winthrop he bought
an island, *Prudence;*
two others, *Hope* and *Patience*
he named, though small.
His trading post at the cove;
Smith's at another close by.
We walk the Pequot trail
as artery or spring.

Wampanoags, Cowesets,
Nipmucks, Niantics,
came by canoe for the games;
matted bats, a goal line,
a deerskin filled with moss:
lacrosse. They danced;
we are told they gambled their souls.

In your apple orchard
legend conjures Williams' name;
he was an apple tree.
Buried on his own lot
off Benefit Street
a giant apple tree grew;
two hundred years later,
when the grave was opened,
dust and root grew
in his human skeleton:
bones became apple tree.

As black man I steal away
in the night to the apple tree,
place my arm in the rich grave,
black sachem on the family plot,
take up a chunk of apple root,
let it become my skeleton,
become my own myth:
my arm the historical branch,
my name the bruised fruit,
black human photograph: apple tree.

Growing Out of This Land

CAMILLE T. DUNGY

Writing Home

When I was a girl-child, home was a street called Bluff View, the uppermost block in a terraced neighborhood of Southern Californian houses. In the summer, when I was young and untired and forced to bed before the sun went down, my lullaby was the view my bedroom window afforded of the hills behind my house. Desert oak, prickly pear, eucalyptus, sage: I fell asleep cataloging this place. In the daytime, I would scramble over one bluff and up the hill behind it, playing teacher in the caves my neighbors and I found, scratching lessons in the chalky sand that lined the walls. We played doctor with stethoscopes fashioned from rocks and the necklaced stalks of wild mustard. We knew the contours and passages of those hills like we knew the halls and classrooms of our other, inside, school. Walking down a slope is different than walking on flat land, and each part of my legs recorded required positions until they could move as correctly up and down those bluffs as my tongue might move over the alphabet. My body memorized its place in those hills.

But even while I lived at the center of everything I knew, everything I knew erased itself. Before I entered high school, construction had begun on summit estates for our town's growing mogul class. The hilltop was leveled and two of my favorite caves lost. From my bedroom window I could now see the red tile roof of the pizza king's palacio. Less desert oak. A weaker scent of sage. When my parents bought the house on Bluff View, our backyard marked the edge of human landscaping. It was not uncommon to find tumbleweed resting in our lounge chairs, to leave wild poppies blooming along the margins of cut grass. Now the hills were asphalt and ice plant. The wild dogs we called coyotes moved down into our backyards, fighting with raccoons over scraps from overturned trash cans and preying on small pets.

Development, in California, means the building of homes, the imposition of landscaping, the digging of pools. Development in California means controlling what exists and creating something new, something only the diversion of rivers for the maintenance of reservoirs can sustain. Development in

California means the mass irrigation of newly planted lawns. Houses, houses everywhere and not a wild mustard field to see. Not even the acres of organized agriculture that first moneyed the region survive. The City of Orange in Orange County kept an orange tree in a fenced area, one skinny-branched specimen saved to represent the fields for which the region was named. I grew up on a street called Bluff View in the midst of California's ambition for development. When I write poems about nature, I am writing poems about loss. I am writing poems about discovering home where home has been replaced by structures I do not want to recognize. The place I was born into no longer exists. I don't have a town I can call home. Unless language is home. Unless, when I write, what had slipped away is found.

Once, I knew the silence and wind-cry of my California hills. In California, the sky speaks with a clipped tongue. Mountains shoulder into the conversation, the ocean sighs in frustration and that frustration rolls over us, is fog. Say the sky and the sea have been arguing all night. Say the mountain blanketed itself and withdrew into silence but the sky and the sea kept at it through the night. Say it is finally morning. When the ocean rolls its wave-blue eyes and sighs, no one will believe the bright points the sky still holds onto. When I lived in California, I was at home in the language of sky and mountaintop and sea. But what my parents came to California to find began to slip away and we moved away as well.

I found myself in Iowa and believed for a long time that I had lost my home. The language of place is a slow speech to learn. Iowa is blue uninterrupted, blue talking all day and a darker blue still talking through the night. Just the waist-high tips of new corn there to listen, and they not saying anything, only nodding their young heads. A new language. I moved to Iowa and didn't write for months. When a poem finally came, it was written in a different tongue.

Now it is half my lifetime since I lived on Bluff View, and I have traveled enough and moved enough to know that home is not a place. I am thinking perhaps home is not language either. Language is too easy to lose. Perhaps home is memory.

It is years later and I am a traveler, walking. I am on public land: a park, a knoll, a meadow. I am glad to own the memories I own and through those memories to belong someplace, to have some place belong to me. I am remembering, and I am writing a poem in my many tongues. A poem having to do with comfort; something having to do with peace. Then a dog comes growling toward me. A dog with still tail and pointed ears. A dog with fanged mouth and purposeful eyes.

The sky is quiet, and the dog is barking, and someone the dog trusts and will obey says, *Sic her, sic.*

If memory is home, I am a long way from hope. I have escaped and am running. I have to remember what has been said: I am black and female; no place is for my pleasure. How do I write a poem about the land and my place in it without these memories: the runaway with the hounds at her heels; the complaint of the poplar at the man-cry of its load; land a thing to work but not to own? How do I write a poem about the land and my place in it without remembering, without shaping my words around, the history I belong to, the history that belongs to me? The dog drags me to fields of memory where I toil from *can* see to *can't.* When I write poems about the land and my place in it, they are informed by this fact: Sometimes the landscape is of little comfort. Sometimes I want to run far away from home.

When I was a child in the hills behind the street called Bluff View, I knew no threat nor fear. Development, the advancement of possession, had not pushed coyotes from the hillside into our backyards. My poems about nature are informed by displacement and oppression, but they are also informed by peace, by self-possession. When I was a child on Bluff View, the dogs we call bloodhounds, the slave trackers' tool, were nothing I knew to remember. I was a girl-child in that kingdom of open space, and all the land I could see and name and touch was mine to love. No one, no thing possessed another, nothing was developed apart from my heart. When I was a child in the hills behind the street called Bluff View, there was no such thing as history. Sometimes my poems rest again in that quiet space, that comfort.

The dog is closer and the woman repeats her command, but it is something all together different this time: *Sit, girl. Sit.*

What place, what words, what memories should I trust? Which direction will take me home?

RICHARD WRIGHT

#559

    Is this tiny pond
The great big lake in which
    I swam as a boy?

The Millpond

They looked like wood ibis
From a distance, & as I got closer
They became knots left for gods
To undo, like bows tied
At the center of weakness.
Shadow to light, mind to flesh,
Swamp orchids quivered under green hats,
Nudged by slate-blue catfish
Headed for some boy's hook
On the other side. The day's
Uncut garments of fallen chances
Stumbled among flowers
That loved only darkness,
As afternoon came through underbrush
Like a string of firecrackers
Tied to a dog's tail.
Gods lived under that mud
When I was young & sublimely
Blind. Each bloom a shudder
Of uneasiness, no sound
Except the whippoorwill.
They conspired to become twilight
& metaphysics, as five-eyed
Fish with milky bones
Flip-flopped in oily grass.

• • •

We sat there as the moon rose
Up from chemical water,
Phosphorous as an orange lantern.

An old man shifted
His three-pronged gig
Like a New Guinea spear,
So it could fly quicker
Then a frog's tongue or angry word.
He pointed to snapping turtles
Posed on cypress logs,
Armored in stillness,
Slow kings of a dark world.
We knelt among cattails.
The reflection of a smokestack
Cut the black water in half.
A circle of dry leaves
Smouldered on the ground
For mosquitoes. As if
To draw us to them, like decoys
For some greater bounty,
The choir of bullfrogs called,
Singing a cruel happiness.

   •   •   •

Sometimes I'd watch them
Scoot back into their tunnels,
Down in a gully where
The pond's overflow drained . . .
Where shrub oak & banyan
Grew around barbed wire
Till April oozed sap
Like a boy beside a girl
Squeezing honeycomb in his fists.
I wondered if time tied
Everything to goldenrod
Reaching out of cow manure for the sun.
What did it have to do
With saw & hammer,
With what my father taught me
About his world? Sometimes
I sat reading *Catcher in the Rye,*

& other times *Spider Man*
& *Captain Marvel.* Always
After a rain crawfish surfaced
To grab the salt meat
Tied to the nylon string,
Never knowing when they left
The water & hit the bottom
Of my tincan. They clung
To desire, like the times
I clutched something dangerous
& couldn't let go.

Seven Pastorals at Sixteen

1
The greying sky and rising wind brings
the evening's percussive cacophony:
thunder unfurls with a crack like a clipper's sail.
The flock knows the way back to the barn.
Through the wood 500 hooves beat dull
down the hard-packed hill path
stream toward the wooden bridge
flow together crossing over two by two.
The clatter of hooves clapping boards
me urging them on from the rear
rams lambs and ewes bleating   baah—   baa—

Over the symphony I think
I hear a plaintive bleat
from over my shoulder.

The lost lamb, leg caught
and cut, tangled in electric fencing,
dies in the night while the rest sleep.

2
Water running over me, I taste
the salt accumulated on my forehead,
washed downstream to my mouth as I run
in a sudden summer downpour.

Crowded drops from the greyed sky
blur the landscape catching the slight light

of the day reflecting sheets of white. Hay bales
grow heavy in the cart I pull.

3
Looking for the misplaced shovel
behind the barn door
opened out to the world
I find a corn snake peacefully coiled,
drowsing, grey and smooth
like creek rocks, his back blotched
with marks the color of the old ploughshare
rusting beside the barn.

4
Snaking, tail and head switching,
body dragging, a salamander left
his signature, just a flourish with inkspots,
drops dripped where feet dipped into mud.

Walking flat footed a raccoon
left birth certificate prints—
impish long toes clawed.

With an opposable thumb the possum's
print that of a mangled hand
a third world infant left in the mud.

A dog's track imprints danger to the flock.

5
The fence is down and the sheep don't notice.
A single wether strays into the space once
electrified and starts—not shocked
he wanders out a ways
testing his hooves on a high wire.
The flock takes note and flows out.

6
Across the pasture the tree
next to the old shack
now bursting with bales of hay
the sweet pears firm hard crunchy
their green skin scarred
mottled and rough against my tongue—
flesh gritty like the old dirt road.

7
Climbing through the barbed wire
fence strung from tree to tree
up the hill out of the bottom
creating two pastures, my brother brushes a barb
opens a mandorla, an almond panel
the intersection of two circles
blood like wine flows free.
Nine years old, he does not whimper—
leans on me down the hill.

Before a Screen Door

Over a darkening spill, water lilies tip,
tadpoles beat against a concrete bank,
and all the banty hens take to their beds
beneath catalpa limbs. Evening comes,
weary evening, and Webster sighs skeins
of clothy smoke, beginning his accustomed
meditation: a wooden match and *Prince Albert.*
Crimp cut. Long burning pipe and cigarette tobacco,
the moments rolled, twisted, and licked with a dull tongue,
while—*swap swap!*—before him, perched
on a weathered edge, his grandchild holds
a fly swatter's stem and plastic slapper,
convinced—*swap swap!*—that she can kill
them all, bluebottle, horsefly, housefly,
flesh fly—all the incessant buzzers.
Quietly, Webster tells her to stop,
then smokes and watches, powerless
before insatiable conviction. Smoke
and splintered wings, these offerings to a distant God,
and in each plastic slap, in each rasping sigh—a psalm.

Skillet,
        muscadine,
                kerosene,

molasses—years later, beside a back door: blowflies,
spring maggots rising from cedar mulch and rot.
I do not wonder whose death has brought them,
or ponder the blossoming flesh, but if they hold

a message, if they whisper *Mercy, O mercy,*
their voices are no stronger than the pleading multitudes.

Skillet,
        muscadine,
                kerosene—yella-burning

in a black night, molasses—these things will attract
flies, sweet things, even death. Believe the body
is a screen door. Believe that peering from behind
the screen is this sign, a little girl in a red dress
and bare feet, a colored girl standing stork-legged
in a red dress. And the fly that bump-bumps
against the screen is also a sign, perhaps corruption
or hunger, a conviction, loss, anything
you can't shoo or kill enough. A fly's wings
are translucent cellophane, divided
like the heart or the tablets of the commandments,
two blades, two tongues, abuzz, abuzz.

Diptera,
        bluebottle,
                blowfly,

housefly, flesh—a child sits before
her grandfather, killing flies. Memory
has a fly's dumb enthusiasm, rubbing its antennae
in blessing or ablution, dropping its sticky eggs
into waste, circling back fiercely, fiercely
trying to forget the touch of so many small deaths.

Pull

I am told it was moonlight that ripened
your failing heart until it finally
cracked, sent the clockhands spinning

off your flesh. I was a coward, still 3,000
miles away, convincing myself that if I
came at all, I could never catch the dying hour.

Forgive me, brother. For decades, your
name has stretched my tongue to breaking.
But love and pain often anguish logic.

Long ago, on a night like this,
I watched uncle rocket a coyote
skyward with a fistful of buckshot.

It slammed to the ground twisted,
skidding across the grass. Somehow,
it didn't know it was dead.

Front legs pawed the air as if leveled
by nothing more than errant moonlight.
Chicken feathers lined its muzzle.

It mewled, eyes tunneling through me
to the underbrush where its mate stood,
cross-haired down uncle's barrel

and already dead by every book and clock.
The mate stood, mesmerized, not knowing
in this world every fool carries a twin heart.

Bang! I shouted and the underbrush
went wild with the mate's running. Still,
if animals have souls, two died that night.

Uncle cursed me under a killing sky.
Why Boy? You know she'll hit
the coop later. Don'tcha know that?

This is my understanding
of the fear and silence
of these wounded nights:

the moon snares in the sweet
spot of the throat. Everything
that lives on is trapped in love.

Two Directions

To me love's an animal, not the feeling of watching one but the animal itself—blunt, active, equipped. The long body and, almost independent of that, the mobile head, the range of its movement, the obvious ambivalence. A horse in the river.

I was a sad boy in a dream on his bicycle in the marshes. Always the first question is Where? Jamaica probably along the Black River itself where the boat takes one to see the crocodiles and then there's a place to eat at the end of the tour where the tour boat turns around at a low bridge. A dream of what?

Love's an animal to me, not working one or the expectation of one's arrival, not "love's animal." Love's full of uncorrected error, the fact of it being unseen or seen and stared at, speechless beneath a bridge, eating with its mouth instead, a croc or any animal.

An island, a river, a bridge. Marshes in the dream, though birdless; and a swaying wooden bridge and the image of a missile having gone up or come up—from where?—through it: I offered it to the boy bicycling as a kind of humorous solace for his situation, an aimless if tangential exaggeration.

(But at the end was a small train station—an archetype—, just out of town, out of the marsh, and going there I got, in the dream, to long strands of passenger cars stretching out in two directions, platforms alongside.)

My Grandfather Walks in the Woods

Somewhere
in the light above the womb,
black trees
and white trees
populate a world.

It is a March landscape,
the only birds around are small
and black.
What do they eat,
sitting in the birches
like warnings?

The branches of the trees
are black and white.
Their race is winter.
They thrive in cold.

There is my grandfather
walking among the trees.
He does not notice
his fingers are cold.
His black felt hat
covers his eyes.

He is knocking on each tree,
listening to their voices
as they answer slowly
deep, deep from their roots.

I am John, he says,
are you my father?

They answer
with voices like wind
blowing away from him.

Mississippi Gardens ✗

slaves, she answers, as I sink
my fingers beneath the roots.

the knees of that blue housedress are threadbare.
she wears it on Tuesdays and Fridays when we tend the flowers.

pullin' weeds ain't a time for talk she chides.
I watch her uproot the creeping charlie.

the fragrant blossoms we protect, hug our whole house.
sweet peas were my choice.

we rarely buy those things for sale in the gardening aisle.
don't make sense to work the earth and not feel it.

I wanted those thick cotton gloves, but they stayed on the shelf.
you gotta learn the difference between dirt and soil.

sometime I notice how the ground changes.

denser, darker, moister, a little more red in some places.

in social studies class I learned about crop rotation

and how it keeps the land fertile.

Mama, what did they used to grow here?

I Called Them Trees

The last time
                    I went to the library
I looked at the flowers
surrounding the statue of Steven Collins
Foster and the old darkie ringing
          the banjo at his feet
                              :flowers planted
in four triangular beds
alternating red and white.
I saw they were all the same kind.

There were others
                    in front of the building
in long wide rectangular rows
bordered by round clusters of pastel green
and white that were too deep, too dark
          red, maroon, for easy images
                              :I called

them all flowers.
And the stunted trees I
wished I had known, bending over the green

terrace above the flowers
          like women whose faces
I couldn't see washing
their hair in deep green pools, I called
trees. If I had told you would you
          have known them?

                         There were
flowers for me. There
were trees. There were kinds
of birds and something blue
that crouched
                    in the green day waiting
for evening.
If I had told you would
you have known?

I sat
          on a bench among flowers
and trees facing
the traffic   surveying all

I knew of impalas, cougars, falcons
barracudas, mustangs, wild
                                   cats,
marlins, watching cars
go by.   I named them
          all.

Beaches. Why I Don't Care for Them

associations: years of being ashamed / my sometimes
fat, ordinary body. years later shame passed
left a sad aftertaste. mama threatening to beat me if I got
my hair wet. curses as she brushes the sand out, "it's gonna
break it off—it's gonna ruin your scalp."
or the tall blond haired gold / bronze-muscled
lifeguards who played with the little white ones but gawked
      at us like we were lepers
sound. the water serpent's breath: a depth as vast as my hatred
skin. my chocolate coating. the rash gone now
as a kid i couldn't stand the drying effect water had
coming out wet, cracked and sore all over. one time
i caught a starfish, second summer after my divorce   → Past trauma
"i'm not into beaches, or riding waves these days." the only time
i like the beach is when it's cold hostile and gray. i feel
kin to it then. or at night. when it speaks a somber tongue
only the enlightened perceive. when the ageless mouth joins
mine. when the soft arms caress in timeworn gentleness. or the
poor man's beach, where bodies echo my chromatic scheme
from just-can-pass, to pitch-tar-black. at home among fleshy
rumps, tummys, thighs,
breasts jiggling a freedom our hearts will never know
sound. eternal splash. a depth as vast as my love
beached. i turn into the blanket. urge him to fuck me. he
thinks it's corny. i get mad. i get up, stomp away, kicking
the sand . . . while he was with her i was on
the beach wishing he was with me . . . at the beach
aware of his hands urgent to touch, take me before we
return to work / our separate lives . . . here, i watch
you swim into the crest. i'd rather sit and sip wine

enjoy the wind than swim or wade. i smile secretly
at thinly clad slappers-on of lotion / a potion to ward off
skin cancer. in my fantasy i would challenge the ocean
a feminist ahab stalking the great white whale. harpoon it
and ride down down to meet davy jones, content
for my america dies with me
sound. swoosh, swoosh the scythe. a depth as vast as my vision
i could live by it, pacifica. learn to like it. now that you're
with me i might even let you teach me how to tread water

RUTH ELLEN KOCHER

At 57, My Father Learns to Grow Things

I prepare to go to the islands,
buy hats, and bathing suits, flippers
that will push even my large body
carelessly through too blue water.
Two thousand miles away, my father sits on his porch,
watches his land, the whole acre
stretched like a small corridor through birch
and aspen sprung from Pennsylvania culm.
He has, just now, discovered the soil,
how it responds to water and spikes of plant food,
tells me by phone each Sunday the inventory of life:
three green tomatoes, radishes, cucumbers,
melons for the grandkids, zucchini everywhere
but the golden ones, not green. Six months before
I visit for Christmas and find myself, 16 and slim,
(a photograph in haste as I cringe at the camera)
there on his nightstand. I'm suddenly struck
by my own absence in his house, even within
my presence—I am gone. Now, while looking
one more time at the glossy magazine of my island,
the stucco balcony where I'll split papayas,
I am jealous of the tomatoes in my father's yard,
the strawberries that ignore their small pots and root anyway
as he protects them with mesh and clanking cans,
turquoise fertilizer that looks like the sea I run to.
I can only ask him to send me brussels sprouts,
carefully packed so the long journey will not cause rot.
I can only savor them when they arrive
like a success between us that closes and opens
the long distance home.

Suburban Noir

Seed crushed. Husk broken. The game unwon
with heads hung low. Turf turned over and cleated,
the bleachered field, en-fenced, is empty.
Sidelines littered with orange peels and puddling
mounds of ice. The good games have all been spoken.
Car doors and the commerce of women with profiles

uplit by taillights and the saplings lining islands
pinwheel leaves like banner wedges strung along
a dealer's lot where late skateboarders abrade the blacktop,
bank and glide like tumbling kites bellying off a last
stratum of air with a kick-step; the rise into silence
and the fall to earth, each rampless lift an undressing,

an uncinching of gravity's saddle and the garment
let go. Electric seawater ripples rec-room windows
in the background through the compound dark
of pine grove and sun down. Beneath a flood light,
a dog's bark breaks across the school's cinder block
where a goal is painted, into which a boy percusses

an endlessly relived penalty kick. Phone poles stake
taut strings through eyelets in the tarpaulin
night lifting lightly at the edges. Condensation
tumbles in the light's slanted dowels, chills
the air against his bare legs.

Letter to the Local Police

Dear Sirs:

I have been enjoying the law and order of our
community throughout the past three months since
my wife and I, our two cats, and miscellaneous
photographs of the six grandchildren belonging to
our previous neighbors (with whom we were very
close) arrived in Saratoga Springs which is clearly
prospering under your custody

Indeed, until yesterday afternoon and despite my
vigilant casting about, I have been unable to discover
a single instance of reasons for public-spirited concern,
much less complaint

You may easily appreciate, then, how it is that
I write to your office, at this date, with utmost
regret for the lamentable circumstances that force
my hand

Speaking directly to the issue of the moment:

I have encountered a regular profusion of certain
unidentified roses, growing to no discernible purpose,
and according to no perceptible control, approximately
one quarter mile west of the Northway, on the southern
side

To be specific, there are practically thousands of
the aforementioned abiding in perpetual near riot

of wild behavior, indiscriminate coloring, and only
the Good Lord Himself can say what diverse soliciting
of promiscuous cross-fertilization

As I say, these roses no matter what the apparent
background, training, tropistic tendencies, age
or color, do not demonstrate the least inclination
toward categorization, specified allegiance, resolute
preference, consideration of the needs of others, or
any other minimal traits of decency

May I point out that I did not assiduously seek out
this colony, as it were, and that these certain
unidentified roses remain open to viewing even by
children, with or without suitable supervision

(My wife asks me to append a note as regards the
seasonal but nevertheless seriously licentious
phenomenon of honeysuckle under the moon that one may
apprehend at the corner of Nelson and Main

However, I have recommended that she undertake direct
correspondence with you, as regards this: yet
another civic disturbance in our midst)

I am confident that you will devise and pursue
appropriate legal response to the roses in question
If I may aid your efforts in this respect, please
do not hesitate to call me into consultation

                                  Respectfully yours,

Homeopathic

The unripe cherry tomatoes, miniature red chili peppers
and small burst of sweet basil and sage in the urban garden
just outside the window on our third floor fire escape
might not yield more than seasoning for a single meal

or two, but it works wonders as a natural analgesic
and a way past the monotony of bricks and concrete,
the hum of the neighbor's TV, back to the secret garden
we planted on railroad property, when I was just a boy.

I peer into the window, searching for that look on mamma's face,
when she kicked off her shoes, dug her toes into dirt
teeming with corn, greens, potatoes, onions, cabbage, and beets;
bit into the flesh of a ripe tomato, then passed it down the row.

Enjoying our own fruit, we let the juice run down our chins,
leaving a trail of tiny seeds to harvest on hungry days like these.

Root

My parents would have had me believe
there was no such thing as race
there in the wild backyard, our knees black
with store-bought grass and dirt,
black as the soil of pastures or of orchards
grown above graves. We clawed free
the stones and filled their beds with soil
and covered the soil with sod
as if we owned the earth.
We worked into the edge of darkness
until everything came from the dirt.
We clawed free the moss and brambles,
the colonies of crab-weed, the thorns
patrolling stems and I liked it then:
the mute duty that tightened my parents'
backs as if they meant to work
the devil from his den. Rock and spore
and scraps of leaf; wild bouquets withered
in bags by the road, cast from the ground
we broke. We scrubbed the patio,
we raked the cross hatch of pine needles,
we soaked the ant-cathedrals in gas.
I found an axe blade beneath an untamed hedge,
its edge too dull to sever vine and half expected
to find a jawbone scabbed with mud,
because no one told me what happened
to the whites who'd owned the house.
No one spoke of the color that curled
around our tools or of the neighbors
who knew our name before we knew theirs.

Sometimes they were almost visible,
clean as fence posts in porch light;
their houses burning with wonder,
their hammocks drunk with wind.
When I dreamed, I dreamed of them
and believed they dreamed of us
and believed we were made of dirt or shadows:
something not held or given, irredeemable, inexact,
all of us asking what it means to be black . . .
I have never wanted another life, but I know the story
of pursuit: the dream of a gate standing open,
a grill and folding chairs, a new yard boxed in light.

AUDRE LORDE

What My Child Learns of the Sea

What my child learns of the sea
of the summer thunders
of the riddles that hide in the curve of spring
she will learn in my twilights
and childlike
revise every autumn.

What my child learns
as her winters grow into time
has ripened in my own body
to enter her eyes with first light.

This is why
more than blood
or the milk I have given
one day a strange girl will step
to the back of a mirror
cutting my ropes
of sea and thunder and spring.
Of the way she will taste her autumns—
toast-brittle or warmer than sleep—
and the words she will use for winter
I stand already condemned.

The Ritual of Season

I. Autumn

The candles we burned each monsoon night in August
stained the wooden holders that kept them in place.
As storm beat mauve to night and night beat mauve to damp morning,
we extinguished fire and bore the day like a crown.

II. Winter

dogged air nipped at our faces
as we lay in formation
along the stiff ground—the young tribe
athirst   waiting mouths open
    longing for snow

daily the heavens held back their glory
    and we swept angels
into hard earth—
donning the silt of adobe wings
        mocking the sun
damning her

III. Spring

      The swollen hum, circadian rhythm,
displaced cockcrow, heralded dawn.

We toured the tan flatland, the ages
    marked in furrowed caverns—
empty, cactus-ridden—sacred
secret paintings the only life
    left on cave drawn walls.

Noon day, come high sun and oasis,
  the headland showed her fury.
Dust would flare and we'd call it devil—
  sheathing our faces, yielding to copper
    coating our skin.

IV. Summer

Under desert sun, road became wavering river.
The shimmer of heat, salamander swift, crossed
the burning middle of July.

When the moon, large as ancestry, conquered the sky,
our weapons were barefeet and laughter—
a porchswing vigil staving off the day.

MARK McMORRIS

More Than Once in Caves

Once, fast along the ridge, we stopped where bush opened
The bones in a pit eager to enter the fuselage of our talk
The swerving of terrain, awake to the measure, the iron of its eye
I tried to pick out the moment when calm went south
And you the girl beside the ridge, a huge breadfruit tree
With balls of fruit, like soccer balls, the pimples are also green
I came from the tree and stood beside you like a vine
To crawl upon the main trunk where the sun sat like Jesus

Once, in deep anguish, the ridge buckled and left us
Steel pipes ran beside the cave where we made fishhooks
Of bone, the debris living with us, a rock with blood on it
The tableau with ankh to protect our backs from the heat
O thief! I went home from the ridge, a mountain lion
Circling the wood pit, the cave was of bone, the fire not yet come
To dynamite the hill as we angled toward its mouth
I waded among the splinters of a water fight, out on Crete

Once, in archipelago, a necklace tied with water, a fuse lit
Brought us into the cave, it shut like a footlocker on our plight
Forced to huddle, we waited for a fire, we sucked gas
And dreamt of smoke and drew pictures of copulation, I went
Beside salt marsh in Guinea, or under stars, of the roof hole
You brought in dyes and set paintings on our left
The rooms lie still, the noise of your breathing in my head
Man in a cave beside a fish bone hook, woman beside a cave

Once, we saw that it was night, the cave opened out of a hill
The rains came, and phonemes sprang new from the ridge
People left for grasses east of the Nile, and I was left

A shell of crab on my back, a crop of wool for my head, gear
Of lights deep over the grass, we ate from each other's hand
Choice meats were stored beside the pit of wood for your trek back
And I took to my bed in thorn, and rain wet me from the roof hole,
Next day we planted out a canefield, I begged you to hand me up

Once, when begging was invented, we sat out the fire and winded
I touched your palm print to my palm for the need of a self
The cave beside a mound of slag, we made hooks of iron from this kiln
The salt mines of Liverpool, the coal pits of Dahomey, the benches
Of courts with smooth bars for the plea, you on the steps
I went up to you when begging was the norm, when the cave was burnt
Poking through the ash, you to the camp of refugees, I to the holding pen
The men went out to plant with their hands what grew in that place

Once, I returned from your neck where my face was on fire
To dig up the roots that grew under earth at the earthworm's back
I picked apples with the daughters of sons, I bought a transistor radio
To you I gave every penny of my sweat till the plantings were done
I looked at sun, straight at it for once, to see if I could stand god's mouth
Went east with the cargo of my doubt, the cave was flooded
We turned back then, to snow beside the hooks made out of our colloquies
There were five of us: two of us were mules, three men in a cave

How easy to be alone when the wind insists, the bones we collect
As easy as digging up the hole, the spirals of talk you make out of wind.

Pachuta, Mississippi / A Memoir

I too
once lived
in the country

    Incandescent
      fruits
       in moonlight
   whispered to me
    from trees
    of
  1950
swishing
  in the green nights

      wavelengths away
       from
      tongue-red meat
     of melon

     wounded squash
   yellow as old afternoons

    chicken
     in love
      with calico
hiss & click of flit gun

juice music
   you suck up
lean stalks of field cane

      Cool as sundown
      I lived there too

CYCLE TEN

Comes Always Spring

MARILYN NELSON

First Skunk of Spring

For most of us the land is no longer our individual partner in the direct transformation of labor into food. Count as a heritage lost the smell of a new-plowed field. Both our traditional relationship with the land and the land itself have become distant. Yet spring speaks to each of us, in a language our bodies first, then our minds, understand. That softening of gust into waft and breeze. Those layers of clothing shed. The cock pigeons strutting and cooing for sex. Squirrel races spiraling the tree trunks. As long as we are able to be out of doors, spring speaks to us of promise, of renewal, of possibility. There are, of course, regional differences in both experience and metaphor. In some places spring happens as slowly as lake ice melts. In other places you go to bed on one winter night, and by dinnertime the next day it's summer.

Here at Soul Mountain, the country house / writers' retreat I am lucky enough to own, I do not work the land, but I do live on it. From my desk I look out on "Peanut Pond" as it changes color. Today the gray cataract of ice has shrunk to only one end of the pond; the rest dilates with reflective depth, a dark portrait of trees and sky. Though I'm still dug in for the solitary Connecticut winter, I can sense the approach of spring. Soul Mountain's spring season starts in March. I'm preparing the house for the arrival of new guests. I look forward to having a houseful of young poets again. I leave the house maybe only once a day now, to check the mailbox up on the road, or occasionally to take my car out of the garage and go buy provisions. The last few days I've heard birds calling from the thicket, and thought, "Oh, spring's coming!" And done a little internal dance.

I remember several past springs. When I was teaching in Northfield, Minnesota, I took my Irish setter, Piper, for several long walks every day. I remember noticing things one spring that I'd never noticed before, and wondering whether they'd always been there and I'd just been blind, or whether the details of this particular spring were different. I remember wondering whether anyone would notice if there were ten or a hundred or a thousand little things that were different this spring, or any spring, and realizing that there would be something new to notice every spring, if I paid attention. Had maple trees always had two kinds of flowers? Why hadn't I ever noticed this before? Were sidewalks littered every March with red bud-covers? I remember feeling that everything was, somehow, more magical than usual, and that I didn't want to miss a thing. The world was changing, growing, unfolding, like an infant who learns several new things every day. That spring taught me the importance of attentiveness to the moment.

I spent one spring semester teaching English in Hamburg, Germany. There I walked almost every day from my apartment near the university to the beautiful promenade along the banks of Alster Lake, where I strolled through the crowds of lovers and families. I was savoring *Leaves of Grass* that spring. Every step I took—on the cement sidewalks of the side streets lined with impeccably kept apartment buildings, and on the white gravel paths of the park, with its manicured greens, white benches, and the lake beyond—seemed, somehow, blessed by the loving sagacity and the soaring verbal beauty of Whitman's poetry. "Who was not proud of his songs, but of the measureless ocean of love within him—and freely pour'd it forth . . ." I feel full of that "measureless ocean of love" every spring. But those spring days on the Alster with Walt Whitman helped me to recognize and name that feeling.

One spring I commuted weekly by plane from my home in Connecticut to a writer-in-residence position in Tennessee. I experienced a double spring that year, and recognized for the first time how clearly chronological the sequence of spring is. As infants follow an almost invariable sequence of development, so spring unfolds with its own inevitability. I would fly out of Hartford as the crocuses were starting, and arrive in Nashville to a riot of daffodils. I would fly out of Hartford as daffodils were assembling their noisy parades, and arrive in Nashville to see stately individual tulips. But Tennessee trumped Connecticut late in the season, with its redbud trees. After their season I was too exhausted from all that flying to be able to notice what flowered next.

I've never memorized the sequence of flowerings. I'm sure gardeners know of its predictable clockwork. Here, it starts with circles of green and white snowdrops growing among patches of leftover snow. Then crocuses bring the first pastels. The trees pink at their branch tips, and skunk cabbage unfurls in the marsh. Then a profusion of bright yellow forsythia. Then the old lilac bushes lining the driveway explode with perfume. Then violets, bluettes, and dandelions in the lawn. I am not a gardener, and I tend to walk through my days in a kind of absent-minded-professor obliviousness. Yet even I notice how each plant comes to blossom at its own time, that it will not bloom out of sequence.

There really *is* a time for everything under heaven. You don't get lilacs at snowdrop time. Spring makes you wait.

I once visited Mauritius and Zimbabwe in September, their spring. It's interesting to see how seasonal metaphors have to be reversed in the Southern Hemisphere. How, in the Christian context there, for instance, an appropriate Christmas metaphor may not be a cardinal on a snowy branch, but an explosion of red flowers on a flamboyant tree. I suppose both of these say something about how light sings into darkness. It's interesting to note that the spring metaphors we use to express the meaning of Easter—eggs, baby chicks, ducklings, bunnies, lambs—are irrelevant in the Southern Hemisphere.

But here at Soul Mountain, spring speaks a language I know. One of the first things I notice and remember with delight every spring is the nocturnal song of the peepers. I know they are tiny tree-frogs, but I've never seen one. Yet the first few times I hear their song, I smile: literally, smile. The peepers say that, even though there's still a skim of ice floating on part of the pond, it's spring. And they say more is coming.

About this time, though snow still lies under the trees and ice still blinds the pond, I start to see moths in my headlights. I start to kill moths with my windshield. The night air, vacant and silent for months, is now full of living things, which I part with my innocent death-machine. But no matter how many moths are taken out by my grille or my windshield, the night fills their absence, closing again behind my hybrid car like a lake closing over a skimmed stone. So earth accepts death, so loss is healed.

I'm not sure which I hear first: the peepers or the returning songbirds. But early in spring I start taking breakfast outside so I can listen to the birds as I drink my coffee. Last year a pair of wrens nested in the little decorative birdhouse I'd put on a wrought-iron plant hanger in the flowerbed just in front of my kitchen window. They fussed a bit whenever someone went out to pull the weeds, but for the most part we coexisted, and he spent a large part of each spring day singing on their roof. I thrilled each time I saw one of the couple leave to fetch and return to deliver food. Life was here, going on right under my nose.

Out here, the countryside is populated. I share my lawn and plantings with deer, my crab apples and pears with deer and coyotes. I watch wild turkeys grow from fluffy black chicks to mature birds wearing widow's weeds and jet jewelry. And though I seldom see them, skunks share our country roads. One of the early signs of spring is a pungent warning taste on the evening air from a distance, or a cloud of vivid stink to drive through with caught breath. Skunks don't hibernate, but clearly something in the spring air makes them get up and follow their noses through the first spring nights. I've noticed something almost pleasant about that scent, when it's faint enough, something almost humorous. My daughter and I have had several good laughs about the skunk's ingenious nonlethal weapon, and wished women could purchase a similarly effective weapon: a stink that one could spray on an attacker, which would stay on his clothing and skin for several days. I love the nonviolence of the skunk, and its freedom to go anywhere it damn well pleases, until it meets up with the Great Midnight Pickup Truck and writes its own lingering epitaph on the cool night air.

The world of experience speaks the language of the Absolute. In that language, the language of the universe, all of the metaphors which spring offers must simply mean: LIVE!

[Earth, I Thank You]

Earth, I thank you
for the pleasure of your language
You've had a hard time
bringing it to me
from the ground
to grunt thru the noun
To all the way
feeling   seeing   smelling   touching
—awareness
I am here!

Bemidji in Spring

In the first city
                                 on the eventually
              Mighty Mississippi
ice fishing
            is
                   day-to-day,
              the ice darkening,
         green
              like a bruise,
                     according to the locals
       —speaking to something
       deeper
                 than the lake. Why not
     money or envy or leaves in deep summer
or my fancy
            far away
                     from this middle place,
         a bit of glass,
         broken wine bottle say,
            cast overboard at sea
                         green against blue
                  tumbling
           back
to shore
        a frosted shard
        because I don't
bruise that way.

At any rate it shrinks,

                   melting from the edges, becoming
    an island to which the gulls
return, shrieking with spring.

NIKKI GIOVANNI

Winter Poem

once a snowflake fell
on my brow and i loved
it so much and i kissed
it and it was happy and called its cousins
and brothers and a web
of snow engulfed me then
i reached to love them all
and i squeezed them and they became
a spring rain and i stood perfectly
still and was a flower

After the Winter

Some day, when trees have shed their leaves
And against the morning's white
The shivering birds beneath the eaves
Have sheltered for the night,
We'll turn our faces southward, love,
Toward the summer isle
Where bamboos spire to shafted grove
And wide-mouthed orchids smile.

And we will seek the quiet hill
Where towers the cotton tree,
And leaps the laughing crystal rill,
And works the droning bee.
And we will build a cottage there
Beside an open glade,
With black-ribbed blue-bells blowing near,
And ferns that never fade.

For Alexis

When I look for you,
I find you among the trees.
They are spirit cabinets
That hold the skin and sinew
Of your soul.

While I pass the giant oaks
With branching arcs
That point skyward,
I hear the rustlings
Of your untried voice
Hushed until springtime.

I walk beneath a canopy
Of willows,
And I am enfolded by the gentleness
Of your wispy arms.

When the redbuds blush fuchsia,
I embrace your coming.
Each year they signal expectancy
And new life.

So when the gray-brown puppy died—

Even after I cradled her in a box
With a heating pad
To mimic the warmth of her mother,

Even after I dripped the watery milk
From a tiny nipple into her mouth,

Even before I could give her a name—

I took her to a circle of trees
To say goodbye.

The trees whispered:
"The Lord gives,
The Lord takes,
Blessed be the name of the Lord."

I stammered out a prayer,
"Our Father, who art in Heaven,
Hallowed be thy name . . ."

Then, you were there,
My unborn child—

I took you in my arms
And held you once.

I nestled you under my breast
And felt the warmth of your blood
Flowing through un-collapsed veins.

I snatched you from the doctors and nurses
Who tested your tiny body for folic acid.

I would not let them put you
Unceremoniously in a jar.

I buried you in a box
Carved with your name—

And the trees took you up
Sucked your spirit into their roots
Turned themselves into *Ibeji*
That I hold in my heart.

For you, I have become
A planter of trees:

The pear tree flowering snow white
For the youthful discovery of your body,

The purple-leafed plum tree
For fertile greening of your dreams,

The dogwood with spotted pink flowers
To decorate the fullness of your years.

So when I look for you,
I find you among the trees.
I count the rings of your life
And watch you flower
And wane
And flower again.

ROSS GAY

Thank You

If you find yourself half naked
and barefoot in the frosty grass, hearing,
again, the earth's great, sonorous moan that says
you are the air of the now and gone, that says
all you love will turn to dust,
and will meet you there, do not
raise your fist. Do not raise
your small voice against it. And do not
take cover. Instead, curl your toes
into the grass, watch the cloud
ascending from your lips. Walk
through the garden's dormant splendor.
Say only, thank you.
Thank you.

Spring Dawn

There comes to my heart from regions remote
    A wild desire for the hedge and the brush,
Whenever I hear the first wild note
    Of the meadow lark and the hermit thrush.

The broken and upturned earth to the air,
    By a million thrusting blades of Spring,
Sends out from the sod and everywhere
    Its pungent aromas over everything.

Then it's Oh, for the hills, the dawn, and the dew,
    The breath of the fields and the silent lake,
And watching the wings of light burst through
    The scarlet blush of the new daybreak.

It is then when the earth still nestles in sleep,
    And the robes of light are scarce unfurled,
You can almost feel, in its mighty sweep
    The onward rush and roll of the world.

JAMES WELDON JOHNSON

Deep in the Quiet Wood

Are you bowed down in heart?
Do you but hear the clashing discords and the din of life?
Then come away, come to the peaceful wood.
Here bathe your soul in silence. Listen! Now,
From out the palpitating solitude
Do you not catch, yet faint, elusive strains?
They are above, around, within you, everywhere.
Silently listen! Clear, and still more clear, they come.
They bubble up in rippling notes, and swell in singing tones.
Now let your soul run the whole gamut of the wondrous scale
Until, responsive to the tonic chord,
It touches the diapason of God's grand cathedral organ,
Filling earth for you with heavenly peace
And holy harmonies.

ALICE DUNBAR-NELSON

Violets

I had no thought of violets of late,
The wild, shy kind that spring beneath your feet
In wistful April days, when lovers mate
And wander through the fields in raptures sweet.
The thought of violets meant florists' shops,
And bows and pins, and perfumed papers fine;
And garish lights, and mincing little fops
And cabarets and songs, and deadening wine.
So far from sweet real things my thoughts had strayed,
I had forgot wide fields, and clear brown streams;
The perfect loveliness that God has made—
Wild violets shy and Heaven-mounting dreams.
And now—unwittingly, you've made me dream
Of violets, and my soul's forgotten gleam.

"Violets" is from *Works of Alice Dunbar-Nelson*, vol. 2, ed. G. T. Hull,
© 1988 by Oxford University Press. Reprinted by permission of Oxford
University Press, Inc.

The Man. His Bowl. His Raspberries.

The bowl he starts with
is too large. It will never be filled.

Nonetheless, in the cool dawn,
reaching underneath the leaf, he frees
each raspberry from its stem
and white nipples remain suspended.

He is being gentle, so does not think
I must be gentle as he doubles back
through the plants
seeking what he might have missed.

At breakfast she will be pleased
to eat the raspberries and put her pleasure
to his lips.

Placing his fingers beneath a leaf
for one he had not seen, he does not idle.
He feels for the raspberry. Securing, pulling
gently, taking, he gets what he needs.

CAMILLE T. DUNGY

What to Eat, and What to Drink, and What to Leave for Poison

1

Only now, in spring, can the place be named:
tulip poplar, daffodil, crab apple,
dogwood, budding pink-green, white-green, yellow
on my knowing. All winter I was lost.
Fall, I found myself here, with no texture
my fingers know. Then, worse, the white longing
that downed us deep three months. No flower heat.
That was winter. But now, in spring, the buds
flock our trees. Ten million exquisite buds,
tiny and loud, flaring their petalled wings,
bellowing from ashen branches vibrant
keys, the chords of spring's triumph: fisted heart,
dogwood; grail, poplar; wine spray, crab apple.
The song is drink, is color. Come. Now. Taste.

2

The song is drink, is color. Come now, taste
what the world has to offer. When you eat
you will know that music comes in guises—
bold of crape myrtle, sweet of daffodil—
beyond sound, guises they never told you
could be true. And they aren't. Except they are
so real now, this spring, you know them, taste them.
Green as kale, the songs of spring, bright as wine,
the music. Faces of this season grin
with clobbering wantonness—see the smiles
open on each branch?—until you, too, smile.
Wide carnival of color, carnival

of scent. We're all lurching down streets, drunk now
from the poplar's grail. Wine spray: crab apple.

3
From the poplar's grail, wine spray. Crab apple
brightens jealously to compete. But by
the crab apple's deep stain, the tulip tree
learns modesty. Only blush, poplar learns,
lightly. Never burn such a dark-hued fire
to the core. Tulip poplar wants herself
light under leaf, never, like crab apple,
heavy under tart fruit. Never laden.
So the poplar pours just a hint of wine
in her cup, while the crab apple, wild one,
acts as if her body were a fountain.
She would pour wine onto you, just let her.
Shameless, she plants herself, and delivers,
down anyone's street, bright invitations.

4
Down anyone's street-bright invitations.
Suck 'em. Swallow 'em. Eat them whole. That's right,
be greedy about it. The brightness calls
and you follow because you want to taste,
because you want to be welcomed inside
the code of that color: red for thirst; green
for hunger; pink, a kiss; and white, stain me
now. Soil me with touching. Is that right?
No? That's not, you say, what you meant. Not what
you meant at all? Pardon. Excuse me, please.
Your hand was reaching, tugging at this shirt
of flowers and I thought, I guess I thought
you were hungry for something beautiful.
Come now. The brightness here might fill you up.

5
Come. Now the brightness here might fill you up,
but tomorrow? Who can know what the next

day will bring. It is like that, here, in spring.
Four days ago, the dogwood was a fist
in protest. Now look. Even she unfurls
to the pleasure of the season. Don't be
ashamed of yourself. Don't be. This happens
to us all. We have thrown back the blanket.
We're naked and we've grown to love ourselves.
I tell you, do not be ashamed. Who is
more wanton than the dancing crape myrtle?
Is she ashamed? Why, even the dogwood,
that righteous tree of God's, is full of lust
exploding into brightness every spring.

6

Exploding into brightness every spring,
I draw you close. I wonder, do you know
how long I've wanted to be here? Each year
you grasp me, lift me, carry me inside.
Glee is the body of the daffodil
reaching tubed fingers through the day, feeling
her own trumpeted passion choiring air
with hot, colored song. This is a texture
I love. This is life. And, too, you love me,
inhale my whole being every spring. Gone
winter, heavy clod whose icy body
fell into my bed. I must leave you, but
I'll wait through heat, fall, freeze to hear you cry:
Daffodils are up. My God, what beauty!

7

Daffodils are up, my God! What beauty
concerted down on us last night. And if
I sleep again, I'll wake to a louder
blossoming, the symphony smashing down
hothouse walls, and into the world: music.
Something like the birds' return, each morning's
crescendo rising toward its brightest pitch,
colors unfurling, petals alluring.

The song, the color, the rising ecstasy
of spring. My God. This beauty. This, this
is what I've hoped for. All my life is here
in the unnamed core—dogwood, daffodil,
tulip poplar, crab apple, crape myrtle—
only now, in spring, can the place be named.

Earth Song

It's an earth song—
And I've been waiting long
For an earth song.
It's a spring song!
I've been waiting long
For a spring song:
> Strong as the bursting of young buds.
> Strong as the shoots of a new plant,
> Strong as the coming of the first child
> From its mother's womb—
An earth song!
A body song!
A spring song!
And I've been waiting long
For an earth song.

Rondeau

When April's here and meadows wide
Once more with spring's sweet growths are pied,
    I close each book, drop each pursuit,
    And past the brook, no longer mute,
I joyous roam the countryside.
Look, here the violets shy abide
And there the mating robins hide—
    How keen my senses, how acute,
      When April's here.

And list! down where the shimmering tide
Hard by that farthest hill doth glide,
    Rise faint streams from shepherd's flute,
    Pan's pipes and Berecynthian lute.
Each sight, each sound fresh joys provide
      When April's here.

Southern Living

I am cut and bruised, my nails broken.
I have found love and my lover is ungentle.
There's a many-hued bruise beside my left knee,
three on my right leg at the ankle and the thigh,
a new-formed scar on my left shin where she cut
me—she didn't mean to. But I fear
I grow obsessed, neglect my looks—my hair
grows wild. This is what it is to love in middle life
and I praise God that She has blessed me
with a love like this before I die.

I lavish this passion on my house and garden.
I have never felt this for any man. To walk
through my own picket fence, to climb
my steps, survey what I have done . . .
the painted ferns and adder's tongue dappling
the shade bed, the azaleas and lilacs
resurrected from the dead, each bed dug
and planted myself, the quartz-hard clods
broken with these two hands, on my knees,
pouring sweat like a baptism—
here I've come to know rapture at last.

The house I had before was small and dark
and I loved a dim, cramped love while I lived there.
The man who shared that space loved nothing
that I loved though in his way he was devoted.
On this barren ground I made my first garden
and watched it fail unsprouted seed by withered stem
by blighted stalk. I fought that soil as I fought

the stony clay of his heart, yet in the end
every precious glimpse of green
went dead brown from the roots.

Let us say the names together:
heart-leaf, barrenwort, rose campion, fairies thimbles.
Feel the meditative music of the names:
Goat's rue, lady-by-the-gate, queen-of-the-meadow.

To love a garden is to be in love with words:
with potageries and racemes, corymbs hispids, and corms.
To love a garden is to be in love with possibility:
for it can never, almost by definition, ever be complete.
To love a garden is to be in love with contradiction:
ravished by order yet ever open to the wild.
But more than all these, to love a garden is to find
your one true lover: for a garden can't survive its maker,
will die with the one who loved it, with only a sudden
spray of roses in June amid a derelict tangle of wood sorrel
and sumac to tell an eye that can read the land
that either of you was ever there.

Geraniums

In my front yard, Negro
flower,

"When Sue Wears Red," Negro
genius behind a picket fence,

nodding heads, blooms
smell spice, not sweet,

burred green splinters,
common weed, edible green—

geraniums in my front yard,
survivors, nigger red.

My Mississippi Spring

My heart warms under snow;
flowers with forsythia,
japonica blooms, flowering quince,
bridal wreath, blood root and violet;
yellow running jasmin vine,
cape jessamine and saucer magnolias:
tulip-shaped, scenting lemon musk upon the air.
My Mississippi Spring—
my warm loving heart a-fire
with early greening leaves,
dogwood branches laced against the sky;
wild forest nature paths
heralding Resurrection
over and over again
Easter morning of our living
every Mississippi Spring!

Fearless

for Moombi

Good to see the green world
undiscouraged, the green fire
bounding back every spring, and beyond
the tyranny of thumbs, the weeds
and other co-conspiring green genes
ganging up, breaking in,
despite small shears and kill-mowers,
ground gougers, seed-eaters.
Here they come, sudden as graffiti

not there and then *there*—
naked, unhumble, unrequitedly green—
growing as if they would be trees
on any unmanned patch of earth,
any sidewalk cracked, crooning
between ties on lonesome railroad tracks.
And moss, the shyest green citizen
anywhere, tiptoeing the trunk
in the damp shade of an oak.

Clear a quick swatch of dirt
and come back sooner than later
to find the green friends moved in:
their pitched tents, the first bright
leaves hitched to the sun, new roots
tuning the subterranean flavors,
chlorophyll setting a feast of light.

Is it possible   to be so glad?
The shoots rising in spite of every plot
against them. Every chemical stupidity,
every burned field, every better
home & garden finally overrun
by the green will, the green greenness
of green things growing greener.
The mad Earth publishing
Her many million murmuring
unsaids. Look

how the shade pours
from the big branches—the ground,
the good ground, pubic
and sweet. The trees—who
are they? Their stillness, that
long silence, the never
running away.

Elizabeth Alexander: "Geraniums" © 2001 by Elizabeth Alexander. Reprinted from *Antebellum Dream Book* with the permission of Graywolf Press, Saint Paul, Minnesota.

Kwame Alexander: "Life" from *360°: A Revolution of Black Poets,* ed. Kalamu ya Salaam with Kwame Alexander. New Orleans: Black Words / Runagate, 1998. Reprinted by permission of the author.

Alvin Aubert: "If Winter Comes, Can Spring?" from *If Winter Come: Collected Poems 1967–1992,* © 1994 by Alvin Aubert. Reprinted with the permission of Carnegie Mellon University Press, www.cmu.edu/universitypress.

Gerald Barrax Sr.: "Barriers" and "To Waste at Trees" from *The Death of Animals and Lesser Gods,* © 1984. Reprinted by permission of the author. "What More?" from *Leaning Against the Sun,* © 1992. Reprinted by permission of the author. "I Called Them Trees" from *A Person Sitting in Darkness: New and Selected Poems,* © 1998. Reprinted by permission of Louisiana State University Press.

Tara Betts: "For Those Who Need a True Story" first appeared in *Gathering Ground: A Reader Celebrating Cave Canem's First Decade.* Reprinted by permission of the author.

Remica L. Bingham: "The Ritual of Season" first appeared in *Ecotone: Reimagining Place* (2008). Reprinted by permission of the author.

Arna Bontemps: "Prodigal" and "A Black Man Talks of Reaping." Reprinted by permission of Harold Ober Associates Incorporated. © 1963 by Arna Bontemps.

Shane Book: "The Lost Conquistador" first appeared in *Bluesprint.* Reprinted by permission of the author.

Paul Laurence Dunbar: "The Haunted Oak" and "Sympathy" from *The Collected Poetry of Paul Laurence Dunbar*, ed. Joanne M. Braxton, © 1993. Reprinted by permission of the University of Virginia Press.

Alice Dunbar-Nelson: "Violets" and "April Is on the Way" from *Works of Alice Dunbar-Nelson*, vol. 2, ed. G. T. Hull, © 1988 by Oxford University Press. Reprinted by permission of Oxford University Press, Inc.

Camille T. Dungy: "Language" and "What to Eat, and What to Drink, and What to Leave for Poison" from *What to Eat, What to Drink, What to Leave for Poison*, © 2006. Reprinted by permission of Red Hen Press. "Since Everyone Can Never Be Safe" first appeared in *Runes Review*. Reprinted by permission of the author. "Writing Home" printed by permission of the author.

Cornelius Eady: "Speed" first appeared in *The New Bread Loaf Anthology of Contemporary American Poetry*, © 1999. Reprinted by permission of the author.

Thomas Sayers Ellis: "The Market" © 2004 Thomas Sayers Ellis. Reprinted from *The Maverick Room* with the permission of Graywolf Press, Saint Paul, Minnesota.

James A. Emanuel: "Emmett Till" from *Treehouse and Other Poems*. Reprinted by permission of the author. "For a Farmer" from *Cosmoetica*. Reprinted by permission of the author.

Jessie Redmon Fauset: "Rondeau" reprinted thanks to the Crisis Publishing Co., Inc., the publisher of the magazine of the National Association for the Advancement of Colored People, for the use of this material first published in the April 1912 issue of *The Crisis*.

Joanne V. Gabbin: "For Alexis" printed by permission of the author.

Ross Gay: "Poem to My Child, If Ever You Shall Be" first appeared in *Ecotone: Reimagining Place* (2008). Reprinted by permission of the author. "Thank You" from *Against Which*, CavanKerry Press, Ltd., © 2006. Reprinted by permission.

Nikki Giovanni: "For Saundra" from *Black Feeling, Black Talk, Black Judgment*, © 1970. "Winter Poem" from *My House*, © 1972. "The Yellow Jacket" from *Acolytes*, © 2007. Reprinted by permission of the author.

versity of Georgia Press. "More Than Once in Caves" from *The Black Reeds* by Mark McMorris. © 1997 by Mark McMorris. Reprinted by permission of the University of Georgia Press.

E. Ethelbert Miller: "I Am Black and the Trees Are Green" from *Whispers Secrets and Promises,* © 1998. Reprinted by permission of the author.

Kamilah Aisha Moon: "What a Snakehead Discovered in a Maryland Pond and a Poet in Corporate America Have in Common" first appeared in *Gathering Ground: A Reader Celebrating Cave Canem's First Decade.* Reprinted by permission of the author.

Indigo Moor: "Pull" and "Tap-Root" from *Tap-Root,* © 2006. Reprinted by permission of the author.

Lenard D. Moore: "A Young Peacock" and "Postcard to an Ecologist" from *Forever Home,* © 1992. Reprinted by permission of the author.

Thylias Moss: "Sweet Enough Ocean, Cotton" from *Slave Moth,* © 2004 by Thylias Moss. Reprinted by permission of Persea Books, Inc. (New York).

Harryette Mullen: "European Folk Tale Variant" from *Sleeping with the Dictionary,* University of California Press, © 2002. Reprinted by permission of the author.

Marilyn Nelson: "My Grandfather Walks in the Woods" from *Field of Praise: New and Selected Poems,* © 1997. Reprinted by permission of the Louisiana State University Press. "Ruellia Noctiflora," "Arachis Hypogaea," and "Last Talk with Jim Hardwick" from *Carver: A Life in Poems* by Marilyn Nelson (Front Street, an imprint of Boyds Mills Press, 2001). Reprinted with the permission of Boyds Mills Press, Inc. Text © 2001 by Marilyn Nelson. "First Skunk of Spring" printed by permission of the author.

Gregory Pardlo: "Man Reading in Bed by a Window with Bugs" and "Suburban Noir" from *Totem,* © 2008. Reprinted by permission of the author.

Cynthia Parker-Ohene: "potters' field" first appeared in *Ecotone: Reimagining Place* (2008). Reprinted by permission of the author.

G. E. Patterson: "April Lyric / All I Know Is," "The Natural World," and "The Mountain Road Ends Here" © 1999 by G. E. Patterson. Reprinted from *Tug* with the permission of Graywolf Press, Saint Paul, Minnesota. "The Sacred

Elizabeth Alexander has published five books of poems: *The Venus Hottentot, Body of Life, Antebellum Dream Book, American Sublime* (which was one of three finalists for the Pulitzer Prize and an American Library Association Notable Book of the Year), and, most recently, her first young-adult collection (coauthored with Marilyn Nelson), *Miss Crandall's School for Young Ladies and Little Misses of Color*. Her two collections of essays are *The Black Interior* and *Power and Possibility*. She is presently Professor of American and African American Studies at Yale University. Alexander read her poem "Praise Song for the Day" as part of the January 2009 inauguration ceremony for President Barack Obama.

Kwame Alexander (b. 1968) is a poet, publisher, and award-winning producer of literary programs. Alexander has written for television and stage and authored eleven books, including *Dancing Naked on the Floor* and *Crush: Love Poems*. He is president of Book-in-a-Day, a school literacy and student-run publication program. He is the producer of the *Washington Post* / Capital BookFest. The Kwame Alexander Papers, a collection of his professional and personal documents, is held at George Washington University's Gelman Library.

Alvin Aubert (b. 1930) is a writer, educator, and the founding editor of *Obsidian: Black Literature in Review*. He has received honors from the Bread Loaf Writers' Conference (1968), the National Endowment for the Arts (1973, 1981), the Callaloo Award (1988), and was the inaugural recipient of the Xavier Activist for the Humanities Award (2001). His poetry collections include *Against the Blues* (1972), *Feeling Through* (1976), *South Louisiana: New and Selected Poems* (1985), *If Winter Come: Collected Poems 1967–1992* (1994), and *Harlem Wrestler and Other Poems* (1995).

Gerald Barrax Sr. was born in Attalla, Alabama, in 1933. He is Emeritus Professor of English, Creative Writing, and Poet in Residence at North Carolina State University, having retired in 1997. Barrax is the author of five volumes of poems, including *Another Kind of Rain* (1970), *An Audience of One* (1980), *The Deaths of Animals and Lesser Gods* (1984), *Leaning Against the Sun* (1992), and *From a Person Sitting in Darkness: New and Selected Poems* (1998).

Tara Betts (b. 1974), a Cave Canem Fellow, teaches creative writing at Rutgers University–New Brunswick. She has received an Illinois Arts Council Artist Fellowship in addition to residencies at Ragdale, Caldera, Centrum, and Soul Mountain. Her work has appeared in various anthologies and journals, including *Callaloo*, *PMS poemsmemoirstory*, *Ocho*, and *Gathering Ground*. She received her MFA at New England College.

Remica L. Bingham (b. 1981) received her MFA from the Writing Seminars at Bennington College and is a Cave Canem Fellow. She was the recipient of the 2005 Hughes, Diop, Knight Poetry Award and was nominated for a 2005 Pushcart Prize. Her first book of poetry, *Conversion* (Lotus Press), won the 2007 Naomi Long Madgett Poetry Award. Currently, she is the Writing Competency Coordinator at Norfolk State University in Norfolk, Virginia.

Arna Bontemps (1902–73) moved with his family from Louisiana to California at the age of three, and in 1924 he moved to Harlem, New York. He published early poems in *Crisis* and *Opportunity*. "A Black Man Talks of Reaping" received a *Crisis* poetry prize in 1926. Between 1929 and 1963 he edited six anthologies and published fifteen collections of fiction, nonfiction, poetry, and children's literature, including *Black Thunder: Gabriel's Revolt: Virginia 1800* (1936), *The Poetry of the Negro* (1949), *One Hundred Years of Negro Freedom* (1961), and *Personals* (1963).

Shane Book's writing appears in U.S., British, and Canadian journals and is widely anthologized. He was educated at the University of Western Ontario, the University of Victoria, New York University, the Iowa Writers' Workshop, and Stanford, where he was a Wallace Stegner Fellow. His awards include an Academy of American Poets Prize, a *New York Times* Fellowship, and a National Magazine Award. The recipient of a Sacatar Foundation Fellowship to Brazil, he is currently working on a documentary film, *Laborland.*

Gwendolyn Brooks (1917–2000), the first African American to receive the Pulitzer Prize in Poetry, is the author of over twenty verse collections, including *Blacks*, *In the Mecca*, *Annie Allen*, and *A Street in Bronzeville*. Other works include a novel, *Maud Martha*, and *Report from Part One: An Autobiography.*

Brooks was named Poet Laureate for the State of Illinois in 1968. From 1985 to 1986 she was Consultant in Poetry to the Library of Congress. Other honors include an American Academy of Arts and Letters Award, the Frost Medal, a National Endowment for the Arts Award, the Shelley Memorial Award, and fellowships from the Academy of American Poets and the Guggenheim Foundation.

Sterling Brown (1901–89), poet, writer, and educator, has three collections of poetry to his name as well as three books of prose. In 1923 he earned a master's degree from Harvard University. He moved to Lynchburg, Virginia, where he taught at the Virginia Seminary and College until 1926. In Virginia he met the poet Anne Spencer and many of the figures featured in his first collection, *Southern Road* (1932). He taught at Howard University from 1929 until his retirement in 1969.

Cyrus Cassells is the author of four acclaimed books of poetry: *The Mud Actor, Soul Make a Path through Shouting, Beautiful Signor,* and *More Than Peace and Cypresses.* His fifth book, *The Crossed-Out Swastika,* and a translation manuscript, *Still Life with Children: Selected Poems of Francesca Parcerisas,* are forthcoming. Among his honors are a Lannan Literary Award, a William Carlos Williams Award, a Pushcart Prize, two NEA grants, and a Lambda Literary Award. He is Professor of English at Texas State University–San Marcos, and lives in Austin and Paris. Cassells was born in 1957 in Dover, Delaware.

Lucille Clifton (b. 1936) has published thirteen books of poetry, a memoir, and more than sixteen books for children. Her honors include the 2001 National Book Award, an Emmy Award, a Lannan Literary Award, two NEA fellowships, the Shelley Memorial Award, the YM-YWHA Poetry Center Discovery Award, and the 2007 Ruth Lilly Prize. In 1999 she was elected a Chancellor of the Academy of American Poets. She has served as Poet Laureate for the State of Maryland and is currently Distinguished Professor of Humanities at St. Mary's College of Maryland.

Wanda Coleman is an award-winning writer honored for her poetry and fiction and renowned for her nonfiction. Her most recent books include *The Riot Inside Me: More Trials and Tremors, Ostinato Vamps,* and *Jazz and Twelve O'Clock Tales.* Her *Mercurochrome* was a bronze-medal finalist in the 2001 National Book Awards, and she received the 1999 Lenore Marshall Poetry Prize for *Bathwater Wine.*

Toi Derricotte is the author of *The Black Notebooks, Tender, Captivity, Natural Birth*, and *Empress of the Death House*. She has received numerous awards, including a fellowship from the Rockefeller Foundation, a Guggenheim Fellowship, two fellowships in poetry from the National Endowment for the Arts, and two Pushcart Prizes. She is the recipient of the Paterson Poetry Prize, and *The Black Notebooks* received the Anisfield-Wolf Book Award. She is the cofounder of Cave Canem, the historic first workshop/retreat for African American poets, and Professor of English at the University of Pittsburgh.

Melvin Dixon (1950–92), poet, novelist, translator, and critic, is the author of *Change of Territory* (1983); *Love's Instruments* (1995, posthumous); the novels *Trouble the Water* (1989), winner of the Charles H. and N. Mildred Nilon Excellence in Minority Fiction Award, and *Vanishing Rooms* (1990); the acclaimed scholarly text *Ride Out the Wilderness: Geography and Identity in Afro-American Literature* (1987); and editor of *The Collected Poems of Leopold Senghor* (1990).

Rita Dove served as Poet Laureate of the United States from 1993 to 1995. Besides her nine poetry books, she has also published a novel, short stories, essays, and a play and received numerous honors, among them the Pulitzer Prize (in 1987, for her poetry collection *Thomas and Beulah*), the Heinz Award, the National Humanities Medal, and the Common Wealth Award of Distinguished Service. Born in 1952 in Akron, Ohio, she is Commonwealth Professor of English at the University of Virginia.

Paul Laurence Dunbar was arguably the first major voice in African American poetry. The child of former slaves, Dunbar was born in 1872 in Dayton, Ohio. His first collection of poems, *Oak and Ivy*, was published in 1892. He read at the 1893 World's Fair where he met Frederick Douglass, who called Dunbar "the most promising young colored man in America." He went on to publish a total of twelve books of poetry, four collections of short stories, five novels, and a play. Dunbar died of tuberculosis in 1906 at the age of thirty-three.

Alice Dunbar-Nelson (1875–1935) was an active figure in the Harlem Renaissance. A writer, educator, editor, and political activist, Dunbar-Nelson published *Violets and Other Tales*, her first collection of short stories and poems, in 1895. *The Goodness of St. Rocque and Other Stories*, published in 1899, is the only other collection of her work published during her lifetime.

Camille T. Dungy, author of *What to Eat, What to Drink, What to Leave for Poison*, has received fellowships from the National Endowment for the Arts, the Virginia Commission for the Arts, the Dana Award, and Bread Loaf. Dungy is Associate Professor of Creative Writing at San Francisco State University. Editor of *Black Nature*, she is coeditor of *From the Fishouse: An Anthology of Poems That Sing, Rhyme, Resound, Syncopate, Alliterate, and Just Plain Sound Great* and assistant editor of Cave Canem's *Gathering Ground*. Her second collection, *Suck on the Marrow*, is forthcoming.

Cornelius Eady (b. 1954) is the author of seven books of poetry, including *Victims of the Latest Dance Craze*, winner of the 1985 Lamont Prize from the Academy of American Poets, and *Hardheaded Weather: New and Selected Poems*. Honors include an NEA Fellowship, a Guggenheim Fellowship, and the Prairie Schooner Strousse Award. With poet Toi Derricotte, he is cofounder of Cave Canem, a summer workshop/retreat for African American poets. He is Associate Professor of English and Director of the Creative Writing Program at the University of Notre Dame.

Thomas Sayers Ellis (b. 1963, Washington, D.C.), poet and photographer, cofounded the Dark Room Collective (in Cambridge, Massachusetts) and received his MFA from Brown University in 1995. He is the author of *The Maverick Room* (2005), which won the John C. Zacharis First Book Award, and a recipient of a Mrs. Giles Whiting Writers' Award. Ellis is Assistant Professor of Writing at Sarah Lawrence College and a faculty member of the Lesley University low-residency MFA program.

James A. Emanuel, poet and scholar, is the author of more than thirteen books, including *Whole Grain: Collected Poems, 1958–1989*, and *Jazz from the Haiku King: Poems in English, French, German, Italian, Spanish and Russian* (translations). With Theodore Gross, Emanuel edited *Dark Symphony: Negro Literature in America*, published in 1968. His honors include the Sidney Bechet Creative Award in 1996, the Dean's Award for Distinguished Achievement from Columbia University's Graduate School of Arts and Sciences in 2007, and a Special Distinction Award from the Black American Literature Forum.

Jessie Redmon Fauset (1882–1961), a poet, essayist, novelist, and editor, received undergraduate and graduate degrees from Cornell University, the University of Pennsylvania, and the Sorbonne in Paris. She moved to New York City in 1919, where she served as literary editor for the *Crisis* from 1919 until

1926. Her essays, poems, and stories were published frequently in *Crisis*, and she published four novels during her lifetime.

Joanne V. Gabbin (b. 1946) is Executive Director of the Furious Flower Poetry Center and Professor of English at James Madison University. She is author of *Sterling A. Brown: Building the Black Aesthetic Tradition* (1985), *The Furious Flowering of African American Poetry* (1999), *Furious Flower: African American Poetry from the Black Arts Movement to the Present* (2004), and a children's book, *I Bet She Called Me Sugar Plum* (2004). As director of the Furious Flower Poetry Center, Gabbin has organized two international conferences for the critical exploration of African American Poetry.

Ross Gay was born in 1974 in Youngstown, Ohio. He published his first book, *Against Which* (CavanKerry) in 2006. His poems have appeared in *American Poetry Review, Margie: The American Journal of Poetry, Alehouse,* and elsewhere. He is a Cave Canem Fellow and a recipient of a grant from the Pennsylvania Council of the Arts. He teaches poetry at Indiana University in Bloomington and gives readings and workshops in various venues across the country.

Nikki Giovanni is a four-time NAACP Image Award Winner. She was awarded the 2007 Carl Sandburg Award for Literature and was the first winner of the Rosa L. Parks Woman of Courage Award. Her children's biography of Rosa Parks, *Rosa*, was a Caldecott Honor winner. Her most recent books are *The Grasshopper's Song* (a retelling of Aesop's "The Grasshoppers and the Ants"), *Abraham Lincoln and Frederick Douglass: An American Friendship,* and *Hip Hop Speaks to Children.* She is University Distinguished Professor at Virginia Tech.

C. S. Giscombe (b. 1950) attended the public and Catholic schools of Dayton, Ohio, and holds degrees from SUNY Albany and Cornell University. His poetry books include *Postcards* (1977), *Here* (1994), *Giscome Road* (1998), and *Prairie Style* (2008); his book of connected essays, *Into and Out of Dislocation,* was published in 2000. He's been the recipient of fellowships from the NEA, the Council for the International Exchange of Scholars, the Fund for Poetry, and other organizations. He teaches English at the University of California, Berkeley.

Rachel Eliza Griffiths is a poet, writer, painter, and photographer. A Cave Canem Fellow, she received the MFA in Creative Writing from Sarah Lawrence

College. Her work has appeared in such journals as *Callaloo, Indiana Review, Crab Orchard Review, Comstock Review, Puerto del Sol,* and many others. She lives in New York.

Kendra Hamilton's poetry and essays have appeared in *Callaloo, Shenandoah,* the *Southern Review,* the anthologies *Bum Rush the Page: A Def Poetry Jam, The Ringing Ear: Black Poets Lean South,* and many others. Winner of an Academy of American Poets collegiate award, she is a Cave Canem and Rockefeller Foundation Fellow, holds MFA and PhD degrees, and is the author of *The Goddess of Gumbo* (2006). She was born in 1958 in Charleston, South Carolina.

Myronn Hardy is the author of the poetry volumes *Approaching the Center,* which won the PEN / Oakland Josephine Miles Award, and *The Headless Saints.* His poems have appeared in *Ploughshares, Tampa Review, Callaloo,* and *Many Mountains Moving.* He lives in New York City.

Michael S. Harper was born in 1938 in Brooklyn, New York, and moved to Los Angeles with his family at thirteen. He attended local schools and lost his innocence in the Terminal Annex of the downtown post office, where he found many literate "friends" working in airmail and biding their time to retirement. He has taught at Brown University since 1970, where he is University Professor and Professor of English. In 2008 he was awarded the Robert Frost Medal from the Poetry Society of America for lifetime achievement in American letters. His most recent poetry collection is *Use Trouble* (University of Illinois Press).

Janice N. Harrington (b. 1956) grew up in Alabama and Nebraska. Her first book of poetry, *Even the Hollow My Body Made Is Gone* (2007), won the A. Poulin Jr. Poetry Prize and the Kate Tufts Discovery Award. She has also written award-winning children's books. After working as a public librarian and as a professional storyteller, Harrington now teaches in the creative writing program at the University of Illinois at Urbana–Champaign.

Robert Hayden (b. 1913) published his first collection of poems, *Heart-Shape in the Dust,* in 1940. He received the grand prize for poetry at the First World Festival of Negro Arts in Dakar, Senegal, in 1966 for *Ballad of Remembrance.* Hayden was appointed as Consultant in Poetry to the Library of Congress in 1976, the first African American to hold the position. He died in Ann Arbor, Michigan, in 1980. His *Collected Poems* were published posthumously in 1985.

Terrance Hayes's most recent collection is *Wind in a Box* (Penguin, 2006). His honors include a Whiting Writers Award, the Kate Tufts Discovery Award, two Best American Poetry selections, and a National Endowment for the Arts Fellowship. He is Professor of Creative Writing at Carnegie Mellon University and lives in Pittsburgh, Pennsylvania, with his family.

Sean Hill, born in 1973 in Milledgeville, Georgia, has received fellowships from Cave Canem, the MacDowell Colony, and the University of Wisconsin. His poems have appeared in *Callaloo, Indiana Review, Ploughshares, Pleiades, Crab Orchard Review, Diagram, Ninth Letter, Gulf Coast,* and other literary journals and in the anthologies *Blues Poems, Gathering Ground,* and *The Ringing Ear.* Hill is currently a Stegner Fellow at Stanford. The University of Georgia Press recently published his debut collection of poetry, *Blood Ties and Brown Liquor.*

George Moses Horton, born circa 1797, lived as a slave on a tobacco farm in Chatham County, North Carolina. Horton frequented the campus of the University of North Carolina at Chapel Hill, where his verses were popular among the student body. When his first collection of poems, *The Hope of Liberty,* was published in 1829, Horton became the first black southern author to produce a volume. His two subsequent collections were *Poetical Works* (1845) and *Naked Genius* (1865). He moved to Pennsylvania after the Civil War and died there in 1883.

Ravi Howard was a finalist for the Hemingway Foundation / PEN Award in 2008. His debut novel, *Like Trees, Walking,* was published in 2007. He has received fellowships and awards from the National Endowment for the Arts, the Hurston-Wright Foundation, Bread Loaf Writers' Conference, and the New Jersey State Council on the Arts. Howard's work has appeared in *Callaloo* and on NPR's *All Things Considered.* Born in Montgomery, Alabama, in 1974, he currently lives in Mobile, Alabama, with his wife.

Langston Hughes, born in 1902, published his first collection of poetry, *The Weary Blues,* in 1926. In 1930 his first novel, *Not Without Laughter,* won the Harmon Gold Award for literature. Hughes was a key figure in the emergence of the Harlem Renaissance and continued as a prolific and prominent literary and political figure until his death in 1967. In addition to more than a dozen collections of poetry, Hughes wrote eleven plays and more than fifteen collections of prose. He also edited several major anthologies and published four books of translations.

Major Jackson is the author of two collections of poetry, *Hoops* (2006) and *Leaving Saturn* (2002). His honors include a Whiting Writers' Award, a Pew Fellowship in the Arts, a Pushcart Prize, a Witter Bynner Award, and a fellowship from the Radcliffe Institute for Advanced Study at Harvard University. Major Jackson is Associate Professor of English at the University of Vermont and a core faculty member of the Bennington Writing Seminars.

Honorée Fanonne Jeffers (b. 1967), a native southerner, is the author of three books of poetry, *The Gospel of Barbecue* (2000), *Outlandish Blues* (2003), and *Red Clay Suite* (2007). She has received an award from the Rona Jaffe Foundation, fellowships from the MacDowell Colony and the Bread Loaf Writers' Conference, and the Paterson Prize for Literary Excellence. She is Associate Professor of English at the University of Oklahoma, where she teaches creative writing.

Amaud Jamaul Johnson is the author of *Red Summer*, selected by Carl Phillips as winner of the 2004 Dorset Prize. A former Wallace Stegner Fellow at Stanford and graduate of the Cave Canem Workshop, he was educated at Howard University and Cornell University. His poems appear or are forthcoming in *Quarterly West, Shenandoah, Indiana Review, West Branch,* the *Virginia Quarterly Review, Poetry Daily, New England Review,* and elsewhere. He is Assistant Professor of English at the University of Wisconsin–Madison.

Helene Johnson (1906–95) published frequently between 1924 and 1935 in such publications as *Opportunity, The Messenger,* and Countee Cullen's *Caroling Dusk: Anthology of Verse by Black Poets.*

James Weldon Johnson (1871–1938) was a poet, novelist, editor, critic, anthologist, folklorist, songwriter, journalist, educator, lawyer, politician, diplomat, and political activist. His anonymous publication of *Autobiography of an Ex-Colored Man* in 1912 is considered by many to have marked the beginning of the Harlem Renaissance era. Among his numerous publications, he edited *The Book of American Negro Poetry* in 1922 and published his own collections, *Fifty Years and Other Poems* and *God's Trombones: Seven Negro Sermons in Verse,* in 1917 and 1927, respectively.

Patricia Spears Jones, born in Arkansas in 1951, is the author of *Femme du Monde, The Weather That Kills,* and the chapbooks *Mythologizing Always* and *Respuestas!* She has received commissions from Mabou Mines for the plays *Mother* and *Song for New York: What Women Do When Men Sit Knitting* as well as fellowships from the NEA, NYFA, the Goethe Institute, and the Foundation for Contemporary Arts. She coedited *Ordinary Women: Poems by New York City Women* and is a contributing editor to *Bomb* magazine and columnist for *Calabar* magazine.

June Jordan (1936–2002), writer, educator, and activist, published twenty-eight collections of poetry, essays, and fiction, including *Naming Our Destiny: New and Selected Poems, Poetry for the People: A Blueprint for the Revolution*, and *Affirmative Acts: Political Essays*. Her honors include a Rockefeller Foundation Grant, the National Association of Black Journalists Award, and fellowships from the National Endowment for the Arts. She founded Poetry for the People at the University of California, Berkeley, where she taught from 1989 until her death.

Douglas Kearney was born in Brooklyn in 1974. Shortly thereafter, his family moved to Altadena, just northeast of Los Angeles. He earned a BA at Howard University and an MFA in Writing at California Institute of the Arts. In the interim, he was honored with a fellowship at Cave Canem. He received a Coat Hanger Award for "Swimchant for Nigger Mer-Folk" and has been twice nominated for the Pushcart Prize. His first book, *Fear, Some*, was published in 2006. In 2008 he was a Whiting Award recipient, and his second book, *The Black Automaton*, was a National Poetry Series selection.

Ruth Ellen Kocher (b. 1965) has authored *One Girl Babylon* (New Issues Press, 2003); *When the Moon Knows You're Wandering* (New Issues Press, 2001), winner of the Green Rose Prize in Poetry; and *Desdemona's Fire* (Lotus Press, 1999), winner of the Naomi Long Madgett Poetry Award. Her work has been translated into Persian in the Iranian literary magazine *She'r*. She has been a fellow at Yaddo and the Cave Canem Workshop. She teaches in the MFA program at the University of Colorado–Boulder.

Yusef Komunyakaa's books of poems include *Gilgamesh* (a verse play); *Pleasure Dome: New and Collected Poems, 1975–1999*; *Talking Dirty to the Gods*; *Thieves of Paradise*, which was a finalist for the National Book Critics Circle Award; *Neon Vernacular: New and Selected Poems 1977–1989*, which won the Pulitzer Prize and the Kingsley Tufts Poetry Award; and *Dien Cai Dau*. His most recent book is *Warhorses* (Farrar, Straus and Giroux, 2008). Komunyakaa is currently Professor and Distinguished Senior Poet at New York University.

Audre Lorde (1934–92) published fourteen books of poetry and prose, including *The First Cities, Cables to Rage, From a Land Where Other People Live, Coal, The Black Unicorn, The Cancer Journals* (which won the Gay Caucus Book of the Year award for 1981), and *A Burst of Light* (which won the American Book Award in 1989). Lorde was Professor of English at the John Jay College of Criminal Justice and Hunter College. She was Poet Laureate of New York from 1991 to 1992.

Clarence Major is a poet and a painter who has also written several novels. A bronze-medal finalist for the National Book Award in 1999, his newest collection of poems is *Myself Painting* (LSU Press, 2008). He lives in northern California, where he exhibits his paintings in several galleries.

devorah major is a poet, performer, novelist, San Francisco Poet Laureate (2002–5), and arts educator and activist. Her most recent poetry collections are *where river meets ocean* and *with more than tongue*. Her first novel, *An Open Weave*, was awarded First Novelist Prize by the Black Caucus of the ALA. Her book of poetry *street smarts* received the PEN Oakland Josephine Miles Award for Literary Excellence. Her third novel, *Ice Journeys*, and fifth poetry book, *war tears*, are forthcoming. She is a featured poet on six CD albums.

Shara McCallum was born in Kingston, Jamaica, in 1972. She immigrated to the United States in 1981 and currently lives with her family in Pennsylvania, where she teaches and directs the Stadler Center for Poetry at Bucknell University. She has published two books of poems, *Song of Thieves* (2003) and *The Water Between Us* (1999). Her poems and personal essays have appeared in numerous literary journals and have been reprinted in over twenty anthologies of African American, American, Caribbean, and world poetry.

George Marion McClellan (1860–1934) was born in Tennessee and lived in Kentucky. A poet and minister, he attended Fisk University and Hartford Theological Seminary. He published *Poems* in 1895 and *The Path of Dreams* in 1916.

Claude McKay (1889–1948) was born in Jamaica and came to the United States in 1912 to study at the Agricultural College of Kansas. That same year he published his first volume of poems, which was followed in the next forty years by numerous collections of poetry and prose, including *Harlem Shadows* (1922) and *Home to Harlem* (1928), a best-seller and winner of the Harmon Gold Award for Literature.

Mark McMorris is a poet and critic whose books include *The Blaze of the Poui* (2003), a finalist for the Lenore Marshall Prize; and *The Black Reeds* (1997), winner of the Contemporary Poetry Series Prize from the University of Georgia Press. *The Café at Light*, a text of lyric dialogue, appeared in 2004 from Roof Books. He has been a fellow at the MacDowell Colony, writer-in-residence at Brown University, and Roberta C. Holloway Visiting Professor in Poetry at the University of California, Berkeley.

E. Ethelbert Miller (b. 1950) is a literary activist and poet born in New York City. Miller is the author of several collections of poems and "arguably the most influential person in Washington's vast and vibrant African American community," according to the *Washington Post*. Educated at Howard University, he was awarded an honorary doctorate of literature from Emory & Henry College in 1996. Miller is board chair of the Institute for Policy Studies (IPS) and a board member of the Writer's Center in Bethesda, Maryland. He is the editor of *Poet Lore* and is often heard on National Public Radio.

Kamilah Aisha Moon (b. 1973) is a native of Nashville, Tennessee, currently living in New York City. She is an alumna of Cave Canem. Moon's work has been featured in several journals and anthologies, including *Lumina, Callaloo, Bittersweet, Open City, Essence, Bloom, Gathering Ground*, and *The Ringing Ear*. Moon received her MFA in Creative Writing from Sarah Lawrence College and is working on the manuscript *She Has a Name*, a collection of poetry themed around her sister's journey living with autism.

Indigo Moor (b. 1964) is the author of *Tap-Root*, published by Main Street Rag (2006). He is a Cave Canem Poetry Fellow, former vice president of the Sacramento Poetry Center, and an editor for the *Tule Review*. Winner of the Vesle Fenstermaker Poetry Prize for Emerging Writers and finalist for the T. S. Eliot Prize, Moor is a graduate member of the Artist's Residency Institute for Teaching Artists. His collaborations include readings with the Sacramento Ballet and Artists Embassy International Dancing Poetry Festival.

Lenard D. Moore was born in Jacksonville, North Carolina, in 1958. He is founder and executive director of the Carolina African American Writers' Collective, the 2008 president of the Haiku Society of America, and executive chairman of the North Carolina Haiku Society. He is the author of *A Temple Looming* (2008), among other books. His poems have appeared in more than forty anthologies, including *The Haiku Anthology* (1999). He teaches at Mount Olive College.

Thylias Moss, author of ten books, most recently *Tokyo Butter* and *Slave Moth,* a novel in verse, is winner of a MacArthur Fellowship, Whiting Writer's Award, and a Guggenheim Fellowship, among many honors, and Professor of Art & Design and English at the University of Michigan, specializing in Limited Fork Theory—the study of interacting systems, whose outcomes are new and (re)configurable forms of visual, sonic, and tactile expression known as *poams:* products of acts of making.

Harryette Mullen is the author of *Sleeping with the Dictionary* (2002), a National Book Award finalist. Her *Recyclopedia* (2006) won a PEN Beyond Margins Award. She teaches African American literature, American poetry, and creative writing at UCLA.

Marilyn Nelson (b. 1946) is the author or translator of many award-winning books and chapbooks, among them *The Homeplace, The Fields of Praise: New and Selected Poems, Carver: A Life in Poems, Fortune's Bones,* and *A Wreath for Emmett Till.* Nelson is Professor Emerita of English at the University of Connecticut; founder and director of Soul Mountain Retreat, a small writers' colony; and the former Poet Laureate (2001–6) of the State of Connecticut.

Gregory Pardlo (b. 1968) is the recipient of a New York Foundation for the Arts Fellowship and a translation grant from the NEA. He has received other fellowships from the *New York Times,* the MacDowell Colony, and Cave Canem African American Poet's Workshop. His poems, reviews, and translations have appeared widely. A finalist for the Essence Magazine Literary Award in poetry, his first book, *Totem,* won the American Poetry Review / Honickman Prize in 2007. He is an assistant professor of English at Medgar Evers College, CUNY.

Cynthia Parker-Ohene is a graduate of the MFA program at Saint Mary's College of California, where she was the Chester Aaron Scholar for Excellence in Creative Writing. Some of her awards include *Callaloo* and Hurston-Wright Fellowships, the Zora Neale Hurston Award from Naropa University, and the Vesle Fenstermaker Poetry Prize at Indiana University, Bloomington. Her poems have appeared in *Crab Orchard Review, The Ringing Ear: Black Poets Lean South,* and *Letters to the World,* among other publications.

G. E. Patterson, poet and translator, is the author of two book-length collections, *Tug* and *To and From.* His writing can be found in many magazines and anthologies, including *Blues Poetry, Bum Rush the Page: A Def Poetry Jam, Poetry 180, Isn't It Romantic, nocturnes (re)view of the literary arts, Swerve,*

Seneca Review, and *Xcp: Cross Cultural Poetics.* He lives and teaches in the Minneapolis–St. Paul area.

Carl Phillips is the author of nine books of poetry, most recently *Quiver of Arrows: Selected Poems 1986–2006* and *Riding Westward.* A Chancellor of the Academy of American Poets, he teaches at Washington University in St. Louis.

Stephanie Pruitt (b. 1979) is a writer and arts educator residing in Nashville, Tennessee. She is a Cave Canem Fellow and member of the Affrilachian Poets. This lover of all things chocolate has published poems in anthologies, journals, and magazines, including *The Ringing Ear: Black Poets Lean South, Warpland Review, Vanderbilt Review,* and *Essence Magazine.*

Claudia Rankine, born in Jamaica in 1963, earned her BA from Williams College and her MFA from Columbia University. She is the author of four collections of poetry, *Don't Let Me Be Lonely* (2004); *PLOT* (2001); *The End of the Alphabet* (1998); and *Nothing in Nature Is Private* (1995), which received the Cleveland State Poetry Prize; and the play *The Provenance of Beauty / A South Bronx Travelogue.* She is coeditor of *American Women Poets in the Twenty-first Century.* Rankine lives and teaches in California.

Ishmael Reed is a novelist, playwright, poet, essayist, songwriter, and jazz pianist. He has won awards in every category and was voted Blues Song Writer of the year by the West Coast Blues Hall of Fame in March 2008. For thirty-five years he taught at the University of California at Berkeley.

Ed Roberson (b. 1939, Pittsburgh, Pennsylvania) is the author of seven books of poetry. His collection *Voices Cast Out to Talk Us In* was a winner of the Iowa Poetry Prize; and his book *Atmosphere Conditions* won the National Poetry Series Prize and was nominated for the Academy of American Poets' Lenore Marshall Award. He is a recipient of the Lila Wallace Writers' Award and the Poetry Society of America's Shelley Memorial Award.

Mona Lisa Saloy, folklorist and author of the award-winning collection *Red Beans and Ricely Yours: Poems,* returned to her beloved New Orleans in 2007, resuming her post as Associate Professor of English and Director of Creative Writing at Dillard University. Her essay "The World Loves New Orleans, but America Has Not Come to Its Rescue" is in *Living Blue in the Red States* (2007).

Tim Seibles was born in Philadelphia in 1955. The author of several books, including *Hammerlock* and *Buffalo Head Solos,* he has been a National Endowment for the Arts Fellow and a writing fellow at the Fine Arts Work Center in Provincetown, Massachusetts. His poems have been featured in *Manthology, Rainbow Darkness, Under the Rock Umbrella, The Autumn House Contemporary American Poets*, and other anthologies. A former workshop leader for Cave Canem, he is Associate Professor of English at Old Dominion University in Norfolk, Virginia.

Reginald Shepherd (1963–2008) was raised in the Bronx. He was the editor of *The Iowa Anthology of New American Poetries* and *Lyric Postmodernisms: An Anthology of Contemporary Innovative Poetries*. His books of poetry include *Fata Morgana*, winner of the Silver Medal in the 2007 Florida Book Awards; *Otherhood*, a finalist for the 2004 Lenore Marshall Poetry Prize; and *Some Are Drowning*, winner of the 1993 Associated Writing Programs' Award in Poetry. He received fellowships from the National Endowment for the Arts and the Guggenheim Foundation, among other awards and honors.

Evie Shockley (b. 1965) is the author of *a half-red sea* and a chapbook, *The Gorgon Goddess*. Her poetry appears in numerous journals and anthologies. Currently a guest editor of *jubilat*, in 2007 she also guest-edited a special issue of *MiPoesias* featuring contemporary African American poets. She is a Cave Canem Fellow and received a residency from Hedgebrook in 2003. An assistant professor of English at Rutgers University, New Brunswick, Shockley teaches African American literature and creative writing.

Patricia Smith, born in Chicago in 1955, is the author of five books of poetry, including *Blood Dazzler*, a chronicle of the tragedy of Hurricane Katrina, and *Teahouse of the Almighty*, a National Poetry Series selection and winner of the 2007 Hurston-Wright Legacy Award. Her work has appeared in *Poetry*, the *Paris Review, TriQuarterly*, and many other journals. She is a Pushcart Prize winner, a Cave Canem faculty member, and a four-time individual champion of the National Poetry Slam.

Anne Spencer (1882–1975), poet, activist, gardener, and educator, was the first Virginian and first African American to be published in the *Norton Anthology of American Poetry*. Her work was widely published during the Harlem Renaissance, and she was a considerable influence on such literary figures as Sterling Brown, Langston Hughes, and James Weldon Johnson.

Amber Flora Thomas is the recipient of several major poetry awards, including the Richard Peterson Prize and Ann Stanford Prize. Her first collection of poems, *Eye of Water*, won the 2004 Cave Canem Poetry Prize and was published by the University of Pittsburgh Press in 2005. Her poetry has appeared in *Calyx, Gulf Coast, Bellingham Review*, and *Southern Poetry Review*, among other publications. Currently, she is Assistant Professor of creative writing at the University of Alaska, Fairbanks.

Melvin B. Tolson (1898–1966) was a poet, educator, columnist, and politician. He was declared Poet Laureate of Liberia in 1947. Tolson published "Dark Symphony" in the *Atlantic Monthly* in 1941, and in 1944 he published his first full collection, *Rendezvous with America*. His epic poem, *Libretto for the Republic of Liberia*, was published in 1953, and in 1965 he published the long poem *Harlem Gallery. A Gallery of Harlem Portraits* was published posthumously in 1979.

Jean Toomer (1894–1967) published *Cane*, his groundbreaking work of prose and poetry, in 1923. *The Collected Poetry of Jean Toomer* was published in 1980.

Askia M. Touré is a poet, educator, and activist. He is a former member of the "Umbra" writers group and a cofounder of the historically eminent Black Arts Movement. He won an American Book Award for his 1989 collection, *From the Pyramids to the Projects*, and *Dawnsong!* won the 2003 Stephen Henderson Poetry Award. He resides in Boston and is a member of the African American Master Artists in Residence at Northeastern University.

Natasha Trethewey was born in Gulfport, Mississippi, in 1966. She is the author of three collections of poetry, *Domestic Work* (2000), *Bellocq's Ophelia* (2002), and *Native Guard* (2006), for which she won the Pulitzer Prize. At Emory University she is Professor of English and holds the Phillis Wheatley Distinguished Chair in Poetry.

Alice Walker (b. 1944) has published numerous collections of poetry and prose, including *Horses Make the Landscape More Beautiful, In Search of Our Mother's Gardens: Womanist Prose, In Love and Trouble, Possessing the Secret of Joy*, and *The Color Purple*, which won the Pulitzer Prize and American Book Award. Walker's honors include the Lillian Smith Award from the National Endowment for the Arts, the Rosenthal Award from the National Institute of Arts and Letters, and a Guggenheim Fellowship.

Frank X Walker, born in 1961 in Danville, Kentucky, is a founding member of the Affrilachian Poets and a recipient of the 2005 Lannan Literary Poetry Fellowship. He has authored four poetry collections: *Black Box; Buffalo Dance:*

the Journey of York, winner of the 35th Annual Lillian Smith Book Award; *Affrilachia*; and *When Winter Come: The Ascension of York*. He has edited two poetry anthologies and serves as the editor of the *Pluck! Journal of Affrilachian Art and Culture*.

Margaret Walker (1915–98) received the Yale Series of Younger Poets Award in 1942 for her first collection, *For My People*. She continued to publish throughout her lifetime, producing numerous books, including the best-selling 1966 novel, *Jubilee*, and *This Is My Century: New and Collected Poems*, published in 1989. Her many honors include a senior fellowship from the National Endowment for the Humanities, the Living Legacy Award, given by the Carter administration, and the Lifetime Achievement Award for Excellence in the Arts from the State of Mississippi.

Wendy S. Walters is the author of *It Wouldn't Be Make Believe*, forthcoming from Palm Press. Her poetry and essays have appeared in magazines ranging from *Callaloo* and *Seneca Review* to *Harper's*.

Anthony Walton was born in 1960 in Aurora, Illinois. He is the author of *Mississippi: American Journey*. He is also the editor, with Michael S. Harper, of *The Vintage Book of African American Poetry*. His poems have appeared in the *New Yorker*, the *Kenyon Review*, *Ecotone*, and *Notre Dame Review*, among many others. His prose has appeared in the *New York Times*, *Harper's*, the *Atlantic*, and the *Oxford American*, among others. He is writer-in-residence at Bowdoin College and lives in Brunswick, Maine.

Afaa Michael Weaver (Michael S. Weaver) is a poet, playwright, and short-fiction writer. Born in Baltimore, as a teenager he worked on an Arabian horse farm. He completed his MA in creative writing (1987) at Brown University and has received NEA and Pew Fellowships and been a Fulbright Scholar. *The Plum Flower Dance: Poems 1985 to 2005* (2007) is his tenth collection. Weaver teaches at Simmons College and, as a translator, works with contemporary Chinese poetry.

Phillis Wheatley (1753?–84), born in West Africa, was brought to America in 1761 and sold as a slave in Boston, Massachusetts. She quickly learned to read and write in English, Latin, and Greek. Wheatley became the first black person in America to publish a book of poetry when, in 1773, her collection of thirty-nine poems, *Poems on Various Subjects, Religious and Moral*, was published in England.

Albery Whitman (1851–1901) was one of the most prolific and prominent poets of the post-Reconstruction era. Born into slavery, Whitman labored until 1864 on the Kentucky farm of his birth and then worked and traveled through Kentucky and Ohio, studying for a time at Wilberforce University. Whitman's books include *Twasinta's Seminoles; or, Rape of Florida, Not a Man, and Yet a Man*, and *An Idyll of the South: An Epic in Two Parts*. In 1893 he read his poetry in the Memorial Art Palace at the Chicago World's Fair.

Sherley Anne Williams (1944–99) is the author of several collections of criticism, fiction, poetry, and children's literature, including the novel *Dessa Rose* (1986) and the poetry collection *The Peacock Poems* (1975), which was nominated for both the Pulitzer Prize and the National Book Award.

Richard Wright (1908–60) was a novelist, poet, critic, short-story writer, and political activist. His influential texts include *Uncle Tom's Children, Black Boy, 12 Million Black Voices*, and *Native Son*. Throughout his literary career, Wright wrote and published poetry, and in the months before his death, he wrote thousands of haiku. A collection of this late work, *Haiku: This Other World*, was published posthumously in 1998.

Toni Wynn's latest book-art edition of nature poetry, *Ground*, is from Shakespeare Press Museum. *Reckoning*, a portfolio about domestic violence with artist Barry Ebner, was published by Editions B.a.D. She is a Cave Canem Fellow and a member of the Squaw Valley Community of Writers. Wynn was born in the year of Oprah and George C. Wolfe: 1954. She is a third-generation Jersey girl who lives by the water in Hampton, Virginia.

Al Young (b. 1939) grew up in Mississippi and Michigan. He is the author of *Something About the Blues* and twenty-four other books of fiction, nonfiction, and poetry. As screenwriter, he has written for Sidney Poitier, Bill Cosby, and Richard Pryor. His honors include Guggenheim, Fulbright, and NEA Fellowships, the Richard Wright Award for Excellence in American Literature, and the Fred J. Cody Lifetime Achievement Award. Appointed by Governor Arnold Schwarzenegger in 2005, Al Young is California's current Poet Laureate.

INDEX OF AUTHORS

INDEX OF TITLES

CPSIA information can be obtained
at www.ICGtesting.com
Printed in the USA
LVHW041915200820
663743LV00001B/25